THE TWEEN BOOK

A GROWING-UP GUIDE FOR THE CHANGING YOU

BY WENDY L. MOSS, PhD
AND DONALD A. MOSES, MD

MAGINATION PRESS · WASHINGTON, DC
AMERICAN PSYCHOLOGICAL ASSOCIATION

Published by MAGINATION PRESS®
An Educational Publishing Foundation Book
American Psychological Association, 750 First Street NE, Washington, DC 20002

Magination Press is a registered trademark of the American Psychological Association.

For more information about our books, including a complete catalog, please write to us, call 1-800-374-2721, or visit our website at www.apa.org/pubs/magination.

Book design by *Hunt Smith Design*

Printed by Lake Book Manufacturing, Inc., Melrose Park, IL

LIBRARY OF CONGRESS CATALOGING-IN-PUBLICATION DATA
Moss, Wendy L.
  The tween book : a growing-up guide for the changing you / by Wendy L. Moss, PhD, and Donald A. Moses, MD.
       pages cm
  ISBN 978-1-4338-1924-7 (hardcover) — ISBN 1-4338-1924-4 (hardcover) — ISBN 978-1-4338-1925-4 (pbk.) — ISBN 1-4338-1925-2 (pbk.) 1. Preteens—Psychology—Juvenile literature. 2. Parenting—Juvenile literature. 3. Families—Juvenile literature. I. Moses, Donald A. II. Title.
  HQ777.15.M677 2015
  306.874—dc23   2014036477

Manufactured in the United States of America
First printing February 2015
10 9 8 7 6 5 4 3 2 1

CONTENTS

DEAR READER,

Welcome to the tween years! When we were your age, the word *tween* wasn't as commonly used as it is today. We were just thought to be at an in-between stage—not a child, but not quite a teenager. However, as you probably already realize, this tween time is a very important time! You are learning to be more independent, more responsible, more mature, and more social. You may be learning about what you now like, who you like, and who you might want to be as an adult. Many tweens even start setting goals and making some decisions for themselves. It's a time of change and possibility!

The Tween Book will guide you as you reflect on being a tween—times when you may feel great and confident and other times when you may feel confused, unsure, and even different. You will read about the ways that expectations—your own as well as those of people around you—may begin to change. You will have a chance to think about what parts of childhood you want to hold onto, and how to find the right pace for growing up that works for you.

This book will discuss how to get used to more independence, and that it is okay to still rely on others sometimes. You will learn how to make decisions and set goals for today and for your future.

Of course, the tween years also involve changes in your hormones and the way your body looks. You will read about these changes, how they may lead you to feel attracted to another person, and how you can deal with these new feelings. The tween years involve more than just changes in your body. Your social life may change, as well. Your friend-ships may change, you may need strategies for handling social conflicts, and may need to know what to do if you are being mistreated socially or even bullied. Lastly, you will read about how to manage new responsibilities at school.

Before we get started, we wanted to mention (and give thanks to) the many tweens who have shared their experiences with us and asked us questions. The thoughts, comments, observations, and questions that they shared are included here. However their names, ages, and exact words have been changed so that our conversations remain private and confidential. While the examples in this book are composites drawn from what we have learned by talking with them, we feel that the experiences and thoughts shared here are common among many tweens just like you.

Ready to begin the tween journey? You have already started by opening up these first few pages of the book! You may find that it is helpful to have your parents or another trusted adult read along with you, so you can discuss these new ideas and concepts. You may find that you learn even more this way. Your parents might learn some interesting information about your thoughts and feelings, too! Enjoy the adventure!

—Wendy L. Moss, PhD and Donald A. Moses, MD

CHAPTER ONE

TWEEN BEING

Here you are! You're between being a child and a teen. You're a tween. But what does that really mean? How does that feel? What has changed? Are you comfortable as you, now that you are a tween? Take a minute to think about how you feel, how you act, and what you think.

DO ANY OF THESE STATEMENTS DESCRIBE YOU?

- ☐ I know what activities and interests I would like to continue pursuing as a tween.
- ☐ I think I can control how fast I change into a tween, then a teen.
- ☐ I have thought about new hobbies and activities I'd like to try.
- ☐ I can balance schoolwork, after-school activities, and hanging out with friends.
- ☐ I am comfortable with the changing feelings I am experiencing as a tween.
- ☐ I am comfortable with the new thoughts and ideas that I have.
- ☐ I am comfortable matching my behavior to the situation.

There is no one right way to feel, think, or act if you are a tween—or a teen or an adult, for that matter! The tween years can lead to some changes, though. You may begin to look different physically, you may want more freedom to make decisions, your friendships and the activities you want to do with friends might change, and you may even find that some of your thoughts and opinions are different now. Some tweens want change to happen quickly, while others like to have a more gradual transition from childhood into being a tween.

Change is an important part of the tween years. It's the time you will move from childhood into being a teen. It's great if you are totally comfortable with the changes that are happening in your life. It's also okay if you are reading this book to learn how to become more comfortable. Welcome to being a tween!

BEING YOU!

Many tweens secretly wonder if they have to say goodbye to everything that made them who they were as a little kid. For example, Zack thought that he needed to pack up his toy trucks and stuffed animals and ship them off to a younger cousin. He thought that he would be teased if he kept these things in his room. Melanie wondered if she needed to stop playing with her dolls and pretending that she was a famous movie star. She was afraid that her friends would laugh at her now if they knew that she still enjoyed both of these activities. Like Zack and Melanie, you have had many years to be who you are. You might be pretty comfortable with that.

So, does everything have to change? Do tweens have to look and act a certain way? Do tweens have to give up the toys and games they used to play with just because they are tweens now? What do you think is the right answer?

The short answer is *no!* If you think that you need to give up the games, hobbies, and activities that you enjoyed when you were younger, think again. Some tweens choose to continue playing as they always have. Then there are the tweens that tell other kids, "I don't play with baby stuff anymore!" and start doing all new things. And there are other tweens who still love all their favorite toys from childhood but only play with them when friends aren't around. Whatever you decide is okay. You can focus on new adventures or stick with what you liked to do as a pre-tween while trying to figure out what you want to do as a tween. It is up to you.

When you make decisions about how you want to act as a tween, you may get pressure from others to "act your age!" Your friends may have certain expectations for how you and they should act, look, and what you should do now that you are all tweens. Your parents may encourage you to try out new activities or take on more responsibility so that you will be prepared for becoming a teen in a few years. Even your teachers may guide you to approach your schoolwork in a more independent manner. Clearly, there's a lot going on during your tweens!

The good news is that you can learn how to deal with these new expectations. Now is the time to figure out who you want to be as a tween, and how to comfortably react to your friends', parents', and teachers' changing expectations of you. You will read more about all these topics later in this book.

KNOW-HOW NOW:

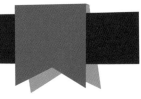

THE ADULTS IN YA

It's not just tweens who hold onto their favorite toys and activities from childhood. Lots of adults do "kid things" too! Do you know why young adult (YA) books like the Harry Potter series or the Divergent series are so popular? Because grown-ups read them, too! According to a new study, a whopping 55% of people buying YA books are older than 18 years old. While you might think that those grown-ups are just buying books for kids, think again. When asked, 78% of those adults said they are reading the books themselves. Adults can have a fun, carefree, and even silly side for their entire lives. Tweens and teenagers may be fearful of acting like a little kid, but really it is okay, even healthy, to hold onto the wonderful parts of being young.

New study: 55% of YA books bought by adults. (2012, September 13). *Publishers Weekly*. Retrieved from http://www.publishersweekly.com/pw/by-topic/childrens/childrens-industry-news/article/53937-new-study-55-of-ya-books-bought-by-adults.html

KEEPING THE "KID STUFF"

Here are some childhood activities that other tweens say they would like to continue doing:

- collecting dolls
- climbing trees
- building with Legos
- playing tag or hide-and-go seek

Can you think of interests or hobbies that you would like to keep in your life as you grow into a teen? You may want to write them down on a separate sheet of paper so you'll always remember them.

You may never want to change some of these hobbies. However, you may want to think about how you could expand your childhood hobbies into "tween" versions of the same interests. For example, remember Zack, who loved playing with toy trucks, and Melanie, who liked to pretend to be a movie star? Zack could start building model cars. Melanie could try out for her school play or go to theater camp.

Here are some more ideas for ways to expand on your pre-tween activities:

- collecting dolls → making clothes for dolls
- climbing trees → scaling rock-climbing walls
- building with Legos → creating building designs
- playing tag or hide-and-go seek → doing scavenger hunts

Now, for fun, can you take it one step further and convert those new activities into adult jobs or hobbies? Here are some ideas:

- collecting dolls → making clothes for dolls → designing clothing or reviewing fashion
- climbing playground equipment → scaling climbing walls → working as a fire fighter
- building with Legos → drawing building plans → becoming an architect
- playing tag or hide-and-go seek → going on scavenger hunts → doing map-making

See? You don't have to change who you are or what you like to do just because you are getting older!

JOINING NEW ACTIVITIES

Now that you are a little older, you may have the opportunity to try new activities. For example, you may be able to try out for a school or community sports club for older kids. Sports teams may become more competitive over the next few years. As a tween, you have the chance to try different sports to see if you want to put serious time into any one of them later.

Being on a sports team can have special challenges in the tween years. For example, Daniel made his school's cross country track team. He loved track and had been running almost since he was able to walk. But imagine how he felt when he walked out onto the track that first day to meet the coach and noticed that most of his friends grew a lot over the summer. Daniel was no longer as tall as some of his friends. At first, he felt uncomfortable and feared that he would lose his edge in track. He talked to his coach about this, and guess what? Daniel's coach wasn't worried. Daniel's speed and stamina were still strong. After talking to his coach, Daniel felt better about being on the team and enjoyed the season.

many communities also have after-school clubs or programs for your age group at the library or community center

Not every tween wants to join a sports team or continue playing a sport at a more competitive level, and that's okay. There are lots of other activities or hobbies to pursue. If you are looking for a way to hang out with a group of tweens, you can try joining a club at school that interests you. Many communities also have after-school clubs or programs for your age group at the library or community center. For example, you could look into joining an art club, theater group, dance program, book club, or other group. Ask the adult who runs these clubs for advice on choosing a program that matches your interests. Ask older kids, ask your parents, ask your teachers…ask, ask, ask! And if you can't find a club that appeals to you, maybe you could start something on your own.

Before picking which activities you want to try this week or month, take a moment to make a list, on paper or in a computer file, of all the activities that you think that you might be interested in. Then review the list, and pick some activities to try now and some to try later.

IT'S YOUR TIMELINE

Some kids wish there were a clear rule book for growing up, something that would let tweens know exactly what to do and what to say…and when. Well, no such book exists. There's no exact schedule, or exact words to use, or exact way to do things as a tween. But that's a good thing. That means you can be an individual and a little creative in developing your own schedule and timeline for growing up. You may have noticed that kids mature at different rates—some girls may be a head taller than every boy in your class. Some boys have deep voices now and others do not. Just as bodies change at different rates, your tween "readiness" happens on its own schedule, too.

> you can be an individual and a little creative in developing your own schedule and timeline for growing up

Each tween's mental and emotional development follows a unique timeline and is affected by individual physical changes, hormonal changes, and emotional maturity. Some of these factors are beyond your control. However, there are some changes you do have control over and can deal with at your own pace. Imagine a boy or girl asks you out, but you don't want to date yet. Do you have control over the situation? Yes. What if your mom now expects you to make your own lunch or babysit for your brother while she runs a few quick errands around the neighborhood? Do you have control in this situation? Maybe or maybe not. In either case, you can share your feelings, thoughts, and concerns in a mature and respectful way.

You may find that you are looking forward to being older and having more freedom and responsibility to make your own decisions. But sometimes, you might want to be taken care of and have things done for you without any pressures or decisions to make. It is not unusual for tweens, teens, and even adults to want to be taken care of sometimes! Remember that you don't have to take on grown-up responsibilities right now. Luckily, you will have time to change from being a child to being an adult. Growing up can happen gradually. Take your time! Determine your own schedule! Consult with your parents and decide what is right for you. Take on some independence, wait until you feel comfortable with it, and then think about moving forward.

For example, as a tween, Samantha started picking out her own clothes and making her own creative lunches. She was comfortable with this increased independence and enjoyed it! Later, when she was comfortable taking on even more independence, she earned money doing extra chores at home so that she could save up for new clothes. When she had saved enough money, she went shopping with her mother. They agreed that Samantha could decide what she wanted to buy, especially since she was buying the clothes with her own money, but her mother would have veto power. Samantha knew that her mother generally trusted her opinions and she decided that part of being mature was to trust her mother's feelings about the clothes as well. Samantha's mother did veto one outfit but generally liked her daughter's confidence, clothing choices, and the fact that she worked to buy these items. Samantha felt pride in being able to buy new clothes that reflected her move from childhood into the tween years!

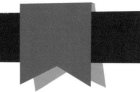

KNOW-HOW NOW:

DISCOMFORT WITH CHANGE

Did you know that psychologists and philosophers even as far back as the Buddha recognize that there are some key areas of suffering (or discomfort) that people frequently encounter? One of these typical areas of suffering is the discomfort with or fear of change. The first step to dealing with this fear is to identify that it exists, accept that it exists, and then find a way to move forward despite this feeling.

Some tweens love the chance to be older and more independent. But did you know that it is also totally normal to be anxious about growing up? Lots of college students are nervous about graduating, entering the "real world," and getting a job. An older adult, who has worked for many, many years may be frightened by the idea of retirement. Changes at any age can be exciting, but may also create worry as you face new and unexplored situations.

Shore, D.A., & Kupferberg, E.D. (2014). Preparing people and organizations for the challenge of change. *Journal of Health Communication, 19*, 275–281.

What would you do if changes seem to be happening too fast for you? Here are a few things to keep in mind:

- Ask people you trust for help dealing with the changes in your life.
- Make decisions that you are comfortable with, not ones that you feel pressure to make just to fit in with your friends.
- You don't have to try every new experience or way of acting. If it doesn't feel right, then it's probably not right for today!
- Remind yourself of why you like yourself and make sure what you are doing reflects who you are.

Don't worry if you don't feel ready to do things that other kids are doing right now. Remember, there's no one timeline for growing up!

TOTAL TWEEN MOMENT: EMMA'S STORY

Emma told her friends that Andrew asked her out. "I was happy that he was interested in me, but I was also kind of grossed out." Most of her friends totally understood her feelings. A few of them thought it was weird that she didn't want to go out with him.

Emma talked to her mom and said that she wasn't ready to date anyone, but she didn't want to hurt Andrew's feelings, either. Her mom reminded her that she shouldn't do anything that made her uncomfortable just to please someone else! So Emma told Andrew that she wasn't ready and wanted to date when she was older and more comfortable with it.

Andrew felt comfortable asking Emma out, but his friend Harry felt he wasn't ready to ask girls out. Right now, though, it can be helpful to just remember that there is no right way to be at this age, so Harry's, Andrew's, and Emma's feelings are normal.

Has this "dating dilemma" ever happened to you?

How would you react if you were Emma?

YOUR FRIENDS AND FRIENDSHIPS

Friends are the spice of your life, the colors of your rainbow, the cheese in your mac 'n' cheese, right? From little kids to grown-ups, many people enjoy hanging out, talking, laughing, or catching up on life with friends. Your tween years are no different. But instead of playing like you did when you were younger, you may want to hang out with your friends and tell stories, talk, or try new activities. Changes in a tween's social life can be scary or challenging to some tweens. It might also be super exciting! A lot of your friends are probably trying to figure out how to adapt to these new social changes too. So, you are not alone!

Sometimes it's a relief just to talk with your friends and try to figure out how you are all dealing with getting older. If you are looking for ways to talk to your friends about some of the changes you are going through, consider these topics:

- Ask what they love most about not being a child anymore.
- Talk about what they miss most about being younger.
- If you really trust your friend and feel comfortable doing so, admit that being a tween can confuse you at times and ask if your friend is confused too.
- Discuss how you all expect to change more in the next year.

You can learn a lot by talking with friends. Your friends might even be relieved to hear that you are wondering about some of the same things that they are!

try joining a club or doing group activities to socialize with friends in person

If you mostly interact with your friends by texting, or on Skype, FaceTime, Instagram, Snapchat, Gchat, or other social media, you may want to add some variety to your social time. In other words, try joining a club or doing group activities to socialize with friends in person, too. When you are in the same room, talking or doing an activity together, you may find out new things about your friend. For example, does your friend have a quick wit in person that doesn't come across online? You may feel closer to that friend when you are sitting together and talking. Also, you may find that working on an activity together, in person, is especially fun!

Lisa spent a lot of her free time hanging out with her friends, talking about boys, thinking about fashion, and drawing with her best friend when she came over. Her parents once said that she was "wasting her time and should get involved in some activity." Her parents wanted her to join a club at school or try out for a sport. What do you think of how Lisa used her time? What would you do if you were Lisa?

Is Lisa giving herself a chance to meet new friends?

Is Lisa giving herself a real chance to find out if she would like a sport or club?

Is Lisa learning enough right now by just spending time with her friends?

You may find that it can sometimes be hard to balance all that you need to do, think about, and dream about, and still find time for friends. But you can find balance with a little planning! There are so many ways to enjoy free time and social time. Talking to friends and sharing feelings and experiences can deepen your friendships, but trying new activities can lead to new interests and being open to new (but safe!) experiences can lead to some enjoyable adventures!

YOUR EMOTIONS, THOUGHTS, AND ACTIONS

If you think about a bridge, with one end being childhood and the other being your teenage years, you are standing in the middle of the bridge right now. You are in-between…that's why you are called a tween! While you are in the middle of the bridge, you may sometimes feel, think, and act like a child at the start of this bridge and sometimes feel, think, and act like a teenager who is leaving the bridge and entering the road toward adulthood. While this is totally normal, it can also be uncomfortable at times. Luckily, you have people to guide and support you as you make the journey, such as your parents, other trusted adults, siblings, and even good friends.

BEING YOU BUT FEELING DIFFERENT

Have you ever been on a roller coaster? Do you remember the ups and downs, highs and lows? Well, you may start feeling like your emotions are on a roller coaster now. For example, Chris wondered, "Why did I start crying when a kid on the bus took my hat yesterday? Usually, I would just tell him to stop and I would act annoyed. Then, I'd get it back. Also, I couldn't even fall asleep last week because I kept worrying about a social studies test. I never used to act like such a baby before."

other people's expectations of you, as well as your own expectations of yourself, may start to change

Actually, Chris wasn't acting like a baby. He was reacting like a tween. As a child, life may have seemed predictable. Now, as you will read later in this book, other people's expectations of you, as well as your own expectations of yourself, may start to change. You may now be interested in making some new friends, learning about different subjects in school, or making more decisions at home. Your family, teachers, and even friends may also start expecting you to act in a certain way as you move through your tween years. These changing expectations can make you feel stressed and more emotional.

Also, you may not realize it, but there are now certain hormones that are making you look older. These hormones can also sneak up on you and make you feel things more intensely. Is that good? Bad? The truth is it's neither! It's something to know and understand though so you aren't too confused about what is happening.

BEING YOU BUT THINKING DIFFERENT

Have you noticed that some of your friends are now thinking in a more philosophical way? This means that they are beginning to ask questions that even adults may not have answers to. Some tweens question information given to them by friends and adults. Some kids look up information on the Internet or research ideas at the library. Some tweens are naturally curious so it's not surprising that they just want to know! Tweens may also start questioning their place in the world, what impact or changes they can have on the world, what job they will get to pay for the things they want as an adult, and so on. Pretty heavy stuff!

Does it help to know that others your age are trying to deal with all these new thoughts as well? Do you have thoughts and questions you'd like to talk about? How would you express your opinions or share your feelings with friends? Here are some guiding principles (that are useful at any age!):

- Make sure you are not making a statement due to peer pressure.

- Think about the consequences of sharing your thoughts or feelings. Are some things better left unsaid?

- Remember that once you tell others something, you really can't take it back, so think before you speak!

- Know that sometimes you learn more about friends after sharing your own feelings and thoughts. If you decide to share your thoughts and feelings, just make sure to leave some time for your friends to also share their own ideas and feelings, if they want.

As you think through big ideas, remember you are not alone. Teenagers and even adults are working on figuring out these complicated ideas, too. No one expects you to have all the answers or solutions. Just beginning to think about these big questions is good for now.

BEING YOU BUT ACTING DIFFERENT

Is it normal to sometimes act really young, sometimes act like an older kid, and sometimes even act like an adult? You bet! You may even feel like there are three different people living inside of you—the young kid you used to be, the older person that you are now, and the person you are going to be. That's a lot of people to live with every day, and it can be confusing to figure out which of those three people to be on a certain day or in a certain place.

You may notice that you also have three (or more) ways of acting. The challenge is to match your behavior to the situation. Imagine if you had a tantrum at your aunt's wedding because you didn't get a piece of the wedding cake quickly. You might understand if adults frown and ask you to "act your age."

Stacey loved snuggling next to her grandmother while they watched TV. Stacey felt like a little, happy kid next to her grandmother. However, Stacey also liked hanging out with her friends and spending time working hard on her school assignments and projects. The third side to her, the side that seemed almost adult-like, came out at times as well when she sat around with her parents talking about politics and world events. If Stacey's brother told her to "act your age" just because she was snuggling with her grandmother, Stacey might have been offended, because she was acting her age!

Take a minute to think about the times when you may act more like a little kid, times you act like a tween, and times you act more like an adult. Do you feel that you match your behavior to the situation?

TWEEN POINTS

- It's normal to be afraid of growing up and it's normal not to be afraid of growing up!

- Most tweens find a way to hold onto their favorite parts of being a little kid even though they are growing up.

- You are still you, even though some things change in the tween years.

In this chapter you learned that there is no right way to grow up. This knowledge may help to take some pressure off of you as you try to figure out how to be you, as a tween. In the next chapter, you will learn about how becoming a tween may change how you want your family members to think about you, and how you might act at home.

CHAPTER TWO

TWEEN TIME IN THE FAMILY

Now that you're a tween, you may notice that the way you, your parents, and your brothers and sisters get along is beginning to change. Maybe you feel that your parents bug you. Or your siblings annoy you. Or you feel like no one understands you. Maybe everything is easy and harmonious and you all get along famously!

THINK ABOUT YOUR FAMILY AND TAKE A MOMENT TO CONSIDER WHETHER THE ITEMS LISTED BELOW APPLY TO YOU:

☐ Adults take me seriously and pay attention to what I have to say.

☐ I realize that I can admit that I don't know some things and that's okay.

☐ I can talk to my parents about how they can better understand me.

☐ I feel comfortable asking my parents questions when I am confused about something.

☐ My siblings and I keep working to make sure we get along.

☐ I sometimes change my mind about how I want my parents to treat me.

☐ I make sure I have some family time and also some friend time.

Being a tween doesn't automatically mean that you will have problems at home. In fact, sometimes becoming a tween makes it easier for you and your family to do more things together. Your family may be able to take trips that young kids might not be able to do, like hiking or backwoods camping. You may have more mature talks about world events or politics, or share more of the family responsibilities at home. Even if you do have conflicts, the good news is that you can probably find ways to work it all out.

> this is a time of change for everyone in your family

This is a time of change for everyone in your family. If you're the oldest, your parents now have a tween in their lives for the first time! Ditto for your siblings. Even if you are not the oldest, your tween years might be completely different from those of your older siblings. Remember this is you as a tween. It's your time. By thinking about (and then talking about) how your role in the family might be changing and whether your wants and needs are different now that you are a tween, you and the rest of your family can begin to figure out how to comfortably relate to each other.

HELLO! HERE I AM!

After so many years being a child in your family, it may take some time for you, your brothers or sisters, and your parents to realize that you are growing up. You may feel that your insights and views should be taken seriously, as seriously as those of adults!

Many tweens are beginning to appreciate the fact that they have some unique ideas to share. Because tweens are growing up and maturing, they may feel that it is time to share their thoughts and be listened to. Does this describe you? Do you want to be respected for your views, insights, and opinions? Here are some things you could do:

- Pick a quiet time when your parents can listen and tell them how you feel.
- Use humor. For example, you could joke and say, "When you are ready for a great idea, let me know!"
- Restate an idea someone else said then share your own take on that idea.
- Show respect for the opinions of others.

Now, imagine that your family is leaving for a long weekend at the beach. Your parents want to leave Saturday morning, but you want to have all day Saturday to jump in the waves and build sandcastles! You might try the tips that you just read about, and then say something like, "Mom, I know you have lots of experience with this, and I agree with you that we probably won't hit traffic if we leave on Saturday morning. But how about we leave around 7pm on Friday night to avoid the major rush hour? That way, we can wake up on Saturday at the beach. We'll be relaxed and ready to start our vacation immediately. I'll pack the snacks for our car ride!"

TOTAL TWEEN MOMENT: DEVIN'S STORY

Devin had a great idea for how to help his grandfather adjust to his assisted living home, but his parents and older sister just kept talking and didn't take the time to listen. Devin started yelling, "You don't listen! You never listen to me!" He then stomped his feet, ran to his room, and slammed the door.

Has something like this happened to you?

Do you think Devin's parents were more likely to listen to him after this event?

Do you think Devin had other choices for how to get his family to listen to him?

How would you have handled this situation?

Tweens sometimes want to be part of adult conversations and be respected and listened to. But sometimes, when adults start to listen to them and ask for their thoughts and opinions, it can cause some worry or confidence issues.

It can feel like pressure to say something "smart" or "grown-up" when someone puts you on the spot and asks you to give an opinion right then before you have a chance to think about it.

What can you say if adults ask you for your opinions and you are not confident about sharing them? You can try politely saying:

- "I'm not sure. I'll have to think about it."
- "I have opinions about other topics, but I'm not up-to-date on this one."
- "Can you tell me more about the situation? Then I can give you my opinion."

Remember that just because you are a tween, it doesn't mean you have an answer for every question. Even adults can't know everything—they need to read up about new topics, ask questions, or ask others for their views before deciding how they feel about a situation. Sometimes tweens start asking powerful questions, such as why people in different countries can't just get along, or what motivates an athlete to cheat or be a poor sport. Even after reading about the question or doing some research, your parents may not have an answer either. If grown-ups are okay with admitting that they don't have all the answers, it's certainly okay for you to do this as well.

GUIDE YOUR PARENTS

You are a guide now. Surprised? You are guiding your parents and your siblings about what you are ready to handle on your own and what you need help with. You can teach your mom and dad that you are growing up and are ready for more independence. It doesn't matter if you have five older brothers and sisters. You are the first you. Rather than leaving your parents and siblings guessing, you can help them figure out who you are.

> you can teach your mom and dad that you are growing up and are ready for more independence

It was probably easier for your parents to understand you when you were young. So you may be confused when they don't "get" or understand you now without you telling them. It's not that they got dumb all of a sudden, and it's not that they don't care. It's that you have become more complicated! One of the confusing parts about being a tween is that you may want independence one minute and want to be totally taken care of the next minute. Here's something that might surprise you: even adults feel the same confusion.

Margo, for example, helps illustrate how parents can get confused by tween behavior. She hugged her parents as she walked through a local shopping center on Monday. On Tuesday, however, Margo was super embarrassed when her mom tried to give her a hug goodbye when she dropped Margo off at school. Margo's parents were never sure if they should hug their daughter or stay ten feet away so that she wasn't uncomfortable. Do you ever change your mind like Margo?

It's important to let your parents know what you need from them and what freedoms you feel comfortable with as you get older. So, speak up. Parents can't read your mind to understand your needs, so you may have to tell them. Here are some more tips for helping your parents to understand you:

- Predict and prepare. Predict what you might need from your parents in an upcoming situation and then talk to them so they are prepared.
- Ask politely. Parents respond better to requests than to demands.
- Explain. Parents can get confused by tween behaviors and need words to understand you.

It's also important to be very specific when you ask your parents for help. For example, James hated when his friend Timothy gave him a punch in the arm as a friendly greeting each time he saw him. James told his dad, and his dad responded, "I don't like hearing this. Why don't I talk to Timothy's parents? I'm sure it will stop." But James wanted to handle this on his own, so he asked his dad for suggestions on what to say to Timothy directly. Once he made it clear that he wasn't looking for his parents to intervene, his parents offered him guidance, without getting directly involved.

you aren't the only one changing

You aren't the only one changing. Now that you are a tween, you may notice that your parents' behavior is changing too. You might feel like they are done "parenting" you, and they really want you to just grow up and take care of yourself. In fact, they may just be starting to parent you differently to prepare you for your teen years. They may ask you to take on more responsibilities, they may sometimes interrogate or question you more, and they may frown on some behaviors that used to be okay.

Becky's parents used to help her empty her backpack after school, and her mom used to sit with her as she did her homework. Now, Becky is expected to do her homework independently. Her mother told her, "School is your job. You have the skills to do your homework or write your teacher a note when you are confused by something. If you have a quick question, let me know and I'll try to help, but I have confidence that you can handle most of your homework on your own."

> your parents may now focus more on making sure you are prepared to be a teenager and then a young adult

You might wonder, "What happened to my parents? Why did they change?" The truth is that your parents are still very much your parents, but the focus of their parenting may have changed. Instead of making sure you have playdates, healthy snacks, and good after-school care experiences, your parents may now focus more on making sure you are prepared to be a teenager and then a young adult. One way for them to help you prepare is to transfer some responsibilities and decisions to you now that you are a tween. They might not be reminding you to do your homework, take a shower, or get to bed on time any more. Parents also know that the world around you may not accept certain "childish" behaviors, even if the behaviors are actually okay in the privacy of your home. So they might be cracking down on things like table manners, email etiquette, or burping, or making other silly sounds. This may be why they seem to have changed. Consider asking them why things seem different. They might be impressed that you noticed!

Sometimes parents may have grown-up concerns that they don't want to tell you about because they believe that they are protecting you. If your parents' moods change, it might mean that they are stressed. They may be less patient. They may not focus on what you are saying. They may even become annoyed more easily, and be short-tempered with you unnecessarily.

If you notice these changes, you might want to gently ask about them. Asking, "What's your problem?" probably won't get the answer you seek. Try telling your parents that you are now old enough to figure out that there is something wrong and old enough to hear about it. Say something like, "Mom, please don't protect me. I'm old enough to hear what's going on."

SEEING EYE-TO-EYE WITH YOUR PARENTS (OR NOT!)

It is very rare for two people to always have the same ideas and goals. Happily married couples sometimes have different opinions. Parents and children have different opinions. You and your friends may not see eye-to-eye. All of this is totally normal. What is important is how people handle these differences.

Here are some tips for working out disagreements while making sure everyone feels respected and listened to:

- Stay calm.
- Communicate respect for their opinions.
- Restate what you heard them say, so they know you heard them.
- Remind them that you are growing up.
- Suggest specific ways you can compromise.
- Give concrete information to explain why a particular situation is so important to you.

KNOW-HOW NOW:

GET A SELF-ESTEEM BOOST

Did you know that having a close relationship with your parents can even be helpful when you are a teenager? Researchers have found that teenagers had higher self-esteem when they felt that their parents were available to support them, were involved in their lives, and had positive relationships with them. So, even though you may want more independence from your mother and father, remember that they are important members of your support team and will be throughout the upcoming years!

Bulanda, R.E., & Majumdar, D. (2009). Perceived parent-child relations and adolescent self-esteem. *Journal of Child and Family Studies, 18,* 203–212.

TEACH YOUR BROTHERS AND SISTERS

Your role in your family doesn't only change in relation to your parents. You are not the little kid you once were and you may now have more in common with your older brothers and sisters. The only way they will know this, though, is by "show and tell." Remember that from kindergarten? When you were a little kid, you would share your thoughts, interests, and prized possessions with the class. So do it again! Go ahead and share your thoughts and interests with your brothers or sisters. You might even ask them if you can hang out together sometimes.

> go ahead and share your thoughts and interests with your brothers or sisters

If you have younger siblings, remember how you want to be treated now, so that you can make their tween experience a good one when they are older. However, your younger brother or sister may still be several years younger than you and nowhere near being a tween. This could be frustrating or annoying to you, especially if they still want to play with you or hang out with you all the time.

When Dina was eight, she loved hanging out with her twin two-year-old sisters. Her favorite activity was playing school with them. Now that she is eleven, she sometimes still likes being with her sisters (now age five), but she often gets frustrated with them. Recently, Dina complained to her mom, "Sophie and Whitney are cute but they can really get on my nerves. They always want to know what I'm talking about with my friends and what I do at school. They try to follow me around, try on my clothes, and even pretend to get onto Instagram like me."

Dina's mom had some suggestions for things Dina could say to her sisters. See if any of these might help you:

- "I love being with you, but I need some grown-up time now too."
- "When I was five, I thought Instagram was boring. It's great if you focus on fun five-year-old stuff. I'll help you with Instagram when you are older and all your friends are on it."
- "I can't be with you all the time, but let's plan special times, just for us three girls."

FAMILY TIME OR FRIEND TIME?

Do you want to share more and do more with friends than with your family? Do you find yourself wanting to share less and do less with your parents? This is common among tweens. Know that when you spend less time with your parents, it can be hard on them. Your parents may miss their time with you. Here are some tips for helping your parents to understand why you are spending less time with them:

- Remind them that there are more activities for you to get involved in now, and you don't want to miss out on them.
- Let them know that you are trying to find a way to see friends and also have family time.
- Plan special family time, such as a game night, so your family knows that you still like being with them.
- Be willing to compromise.

By talking through the issue with your parents, and being willing to compromise and make time for them, you can help them understand you better. They may even be impressed with your maturity!

REMEMBER THIS:
YOU CAN CHANGE YOUR MIND

Have you ever noticed that you change your mind a lot about how you want to be treated, what you want to do, and even how you feel? The tween years are all about change, so this isn't surprising, but can be confusing to you and to the people around you.

If you find that you are changing your mind, it's okay to let your parents or your siblings know that you realize that you do this sometimes and that you aren't purposely trying to confuse them. Remember when Margo wanted to hug her parents at the shopping center one day, but then was embarrassed when her mom hugged her another day? Like Margo, you might feel differently about the same situation at different times. Because you are a tween, you may sometimes feel more like a child and sometimes feel more like a teen. If you talk about this with your parents or your older siblings, they might understand more than you expect—after all, they were once tweens too! Even younger brothers and sisters might understand if you calmly explain it to them. Remember, you have a right to change your mind, and change it again soon after. Just let others know what's going on.

TOTAL TWEEN MOMENT: ROB'S STORY

Twelve-year-old Rob found that he was always arguing with his parents. He wanted to be able to make decisions for himself and be independent. He felt that his parents were always trying to tell him what to do and always wanted to know where he was and who he was with. He was angry when they told him to do his chores, when they asked him to join them for dinner, and when they asked him to take showers each night. When Rob started going to after-school clubs and spending a lot of time with his friends, his parents felt left out. One night, his parents said, "We miss our Robby. Why don't the three of us plan something to do together?" Rob later told his friend, "I thought they would have been happy not to have me around so much. Who knew that they missed me?!"

Rob first asked his parents not to call him Robby anymore, because now that he is older he prefers being called Rob. He and his parents also agreed that he should have more chances to make decisions for himself, but that his parents still needed to be his "co-pilots" and help him to make the best decisions for himself now and for his future. After they talked, Rob realized that his parents were being flexible and giving him more control of his life, but also trying to guide him through his tween years.

Does Rob's story sound familiar?

Do you think a discussion similar to the one Rob had would work for you and your parents?

Has anything like this happened to you?

If so, how did you work it out with your family?

TWEEN POINTS

- You have the power to teach others about yourself. Give it a try!

- Tweens often want to be taken seriously and be heard.

- Tweens, parents, and siblings are all trying to figure out how things are changing.

In this chapter, you read about how tweens often want to be taken seriously. You also learned some ways to communicate your needs and wants to your parents and siblings. What if you want your parents to grant you more independence? In the next chapter, you will read about some steps you can take to gain more independence and take on new challenges.

CHAPTER THREE

TWEEN INDEPENDENCE

Many tweens say that they can't wait until they can be totally independent and make all their own decisions. But a lot of tweens also worry about having too much pressure, responsibility, and independence. They may be concerned that their parents won't help them out anymore, that they won't be able to handle things on their own, or that they will feel overwhelmed with decisions.

HOW DO YOU FEEL? TAKE A MOMENT TO READ THROUGH THE ITEMS BELOW. DO ANY OF THESE STATEMENTS DESCRIBE YOU?

☐ I understand what it means to become more independent.

☐ I know when I need to ask others for help.

☐ I feel confident handling new experiences and I can forgive myself for my mistakes.

☐ I don't let others take over when I know I can do something myself.

☐ I know how to prove to my parents that I'm ready to handle more independence.

☐ I am not afraid to discuss my views and opinions, when it's appropriate.

This chapter will teach you how to talk with your parents about your desire for more independence as well as your fears. You will learn that it's okay to ask for help when you need it. You will also read about becoming an independent thinker.

TO BE INDEPENDENT (OR NOT?!)

Sometimes tweens think that becoming independent from their parents means that they don't need to rely on anyone anymore. As a tween, independence just means that you have more freedom to handle situations on your own and can take on more responsibility. This might come in the form of ordering food on your own at a restaurant or coming home from school by yourself. If you want to gain and keep your independence, the first thing you need to do is figure out when you can responsibly handle situations on your own and when you may still need help from others.

The truth is that no one is totally independent. Adults depend on other people all the time. Your teacher may ask the school psychologist for ways to help a student who is stressed out and has trouble taking tests. Your dad may turn to a mechanic to ask for help fixing his car. Your older brother or sister may ask the soccer coach how to stretch properly after a hard practice. It is actually wise to realize that others may sometimes have more knowledge or skills than you do! It shows emotional strength and courage to be able to ask for help from these people. So if you need guidance, ask for this help.

How about you? Do you know when to ask for help? It is difficult to figure out how to balance asking for help and relying on yourself. Here are some tips:

- Ask yourself what the worst thing is that could happen if you try to handle the situation on your own. If the worst is seriously bad, it might be time to get help!

- Be realistic—remember that everyone needs someone sometimes and everyone wants to be taken care of once in a while.

- Ask yourself if you can deal with the situation on your own, but would rather be taken care of. It's okay to let others take care of you *sometimes!*

- Realize that you don't have to be independent all at once. Maturity is about picking the right time to do more on your own and finding the right time to get help.

Taking small steps toward independence can be fun if you understand that feeling challenged by obstacles you may encounter doesn't mean that you are not a capable, maturing person.

Matthew said, "At first I thought that if I messed up, then I was a mess-up. After talking with my parents, I know I still want to have them help me out with big things, but if I try new experiences and don't succeed, it doesn't mean I'm not a success. My mom said that I'm a success anyway because I had the courage to try to handle a new situation."

What about you? Do you feel confident enough to ask for help when needed, enjoy the journey of learning, and forgive yourself for mistakes?

KNOW-HOW NOW:

EASING INTO INDEPENDENCE

Did you know that parents often treat kids differently depending on their age? In a study of 110 families, a researcher looked at parenting styles for raising 11-, 14-, and 17-year-olds. Guess what? She found that parents of 17-year-olds, as compared to parents of 11- or 14-year-olds, gave these teenagers more freedom to make independent decisions.

Does this surprise you? Your parents will probably slowly ease you into more and more independence. So you're not alone and you can gradually get used to this!

It's okay to ask your parents for help, so you are ready to make decisions more independently as you get older.

Newman, B.M. (1989). The changing nature of the parent-adolescent relationship from early to late adolescence. *Adolescence, 24*, 915–924.

Zoe didn't want her parents to always tell her when to go to bed, when to do her homework, when to get off Instagram, and when to wake up. So she came up with a plan to show her parents that she was no longer a little kid and shouldn't be treated like one.

Zoe asked for a family meeting with both her mother and father, and used this time to talk about things she wanted to change. Zoe and her parents calmly talked and they eventually all agreed on the following plan: Zoe could change her bedtime to 9pm and decide what time to wake up as long as she was able to do her morning chores and catch her school bus without any problems. Zoe was allowed to try doing her homework whenever she wanted, but if her grades dropped this plan would be cancelled. As far as Instagram, her parents didn't budge. They believed that it was important to closely supervise what she did on Instagram and they didn't want her on it for more than a short time each day, partly because they wanted her to join family activities and not just focus on her iPad.

Even though she didn't get everything she asked for, Zoe was happy that her parents at least listened to her, and that she did get the later bedtime, the chance to do her homework when she wanted, and the freedom to decide when to wake up. All she needed to do was keep her part of the bargain—do her morning chores, catch the bus each morning, and keep her grades up.

What do you think?

Who won, Zoe or her parents? Neither? Both? Did they all compromise?

Do you think this plan would work in your family?

TO DECLARE YOUR INDEPENDENCE

Did you ever want to set your own bedtime? Decide when (or if) you will brush your teeth? As you get older, you may want to make more of your own decisions about the things that you do every day. The question is, will your parents go along with that plan?

Part of growing up and being independent is learning to compromise. Even though your parents might not agree to everything you want, there are ways to demonstrate to them that you are ready for more independence. Here are some tips:

- Ask to take on more responsibility to prove you can be reliable.
- Make sure that you do the things you need to do before your parents tell you to do them.
- Ask your parents what they need, rather than thinking only about what you want.
- Make sure you remember to do your schoolwork.
- Show people outside your house, such as your teachers and your friends' parents, that you are thoughtful and polite.
- Join in family conversations to show your parents that you have your own opinions and thoughts to share.

But wait. What if your parents make it super easy for you to be taken care of by them? What if they really want to help you manage all of your problems? Sounds good, right? Well, maybe not. Parents generally want to protect you from pain and struggles. But, if they totally protect you, you may never gain the confidence to know that you can be independent. For example, Seth was building a model airplane at the workbench in the basement of his home. His father saw that he was struggling to glue two small pieces of the plane together. He said, "Seth, let me help you with this." He took the two pieces, glued them together, and handed them back to Seth. He then sat down next to his son and started working on other parts of the plane, even though Seth said he wanted to do it on his own.

> next time your parents offer help, take a moment to decide whether you need their help

How do you think Seth felt about his dad's help? Do you think he was annoyed that his father took over when he wanted to build the model airplane on his own?

While some tweens are relieved to have parents that totally take care of them, this can become a problem as you get older if you never allow yourself to take on more responsibility, challenges, and stress. If this is the case for you, next time your parents offer help, take a moment to decide whether you need their help or if you can learn more from managing the task independently.

On the other hand, if you have parents who encourage you to do things on your own, you may sometimes feel nervous or even annoyed that they won't fix every problem or take care of every challenge that you face. Nicole was baking cupcakes with her mom for her birthday celebration in school. When her mother asked her to measure the ingredients and mix them, Nicole said that she didn't want to do this because she was worried that she might make a mistake. Her mother calmly explained, "I know you can do this. I'm right here if you have questions, but give it a try. What's the worst that can happen?" Nicole nodded, tried it, and felt proud of herself when she realized she had taken on a new task and done it well!

> take a moment to decide whether you need your parents' help or if you can learn more from managing the task independently

Every once in a while, it might be helpful to talk with your parents about times when you feel they don't let you be independent, when you feel that they ask you to be too independent, and when you feel comfortable with how things are going. Then you can hear why they made the choices they did, and you and your parents can understand each other better. Give it a try!

TO THINK FOR YOURSELF

In addition to taking on more responsibility and handling more situations on your own, it's time now to start thinking more independently. Being an independent thinker allows you to have new ideas, creative thoughts, and unique perspectives, as well as the opportunity to be a leader, not a follower!

You may have already noticed that you are not always thinking like your friends, parents, or even your teachers. You may also realize that some thoughts are great to share and some may be better kept to yourself. Abby was hanging out at her friend Tatum's house when she thought, "I like Tatum, but I do more fun stuff with Sheila and Mae. I wish

I was with Sheila and Mae today at the street fair." If Abby told Tatum how she felt, Tatum's feelings might have been hurt. So instead, Abby decided to filter her thoughts, which means she decided to keep them in her head rather than share them with Tatum. Abby thought, "I wonder if I should invite Sheila and Mae to go with me and Tatum to the next street fair? I think that would be fun for everyone!"

Talk to people you trust to share your ideas and get their reactions. They may not always agree with your opinions, but hopefully they will be interested in what you have to say,

> talk to people you trust to share your ideas and get their reactions

and respectful of your views (and you can be respectful of theirs, as well). At times, you may want to explain or even defend your ideas. Imagine if a very young Bill Gates shared his ideas for computer programming and software with other very bright people who did not believe that computers would ever play a significant part in everyday life. It would take courage and confidence to stick to his goals, and patience to explain his ideas.

Sometimes it's tricky to decide whether to share what you're thinking. Here is a good strategy to help you decide when, where, and how to share your thoughts:

- *When?* Pick a time when others have time to listen to you, you are not interrupting others with a new conversation, and there are not people there who would be hurt or offended. However, if you need to confront someone and she might be hurt— for example, if you feel it's important to tell a friend that her idea for the theme of the dance is not the best choice—prepare her, be respectful, and try to reduce the chances of making the other person feel uncomfortable.

- *Where?* There are some places where it's okay to share different opinions and ideas and some where it is not. At the dinner table, some families set aside time to discuss thoughts and views. However, at a baseball game, it's probably not a good idea to go over to a group of people wearing the opposing team's shirts and start explaining to them why their team isn't as good as the team you support.

- *How?* Carefully! Respectfully! Gently! It's always helpful to make it clear that you can respect other opinions but you are just explaining how you feel or are reacting to a situation.

Even if you pick the right *when, where,* and *how,* some topics often create tensions, such as drugs, politics, and religion. Be prepared for some people to disagree or to become emotional in response to your opinions on these topics.

Without independent and creative thought, we may not have some of history's most amazing inventions. We would not have electricity and airplanes would never have left the ground! As a tween, you have the amazing opportunity to think about the future and how your thoughts, ideas, and actions can shape it. Being able to imagine what is not obvious is a sign of an independent thinker!

Take a moment to think about your own unique, creative thoughts and ideas. When you realize that you are having independent thoughts, write them down. You may want to put them all in a journal. This way, you can remember to share your ideas, or add to them, later.

TOTAL TWEEN MOMENT: **PAUL'S STORY**

Paul interrupted his teacher's art lesson and said, "You always talk about these artists like they are rock stars and like they changed the world." Paul then added, "Sure, some of these people are talented, but they don't change history or change the world. Why do you care about this stuff anyway?" Paul's teacher told him that his ideas were interesting and that they could talk about them after class, but that he was "interrupting the lesson right now."

Did Paul have a right to share his thoughts during art class?

Did Paul have a right to express his views?

How could Paul have handled this differently?

What would you have done if you were Paul?

TWEEN
POINTS

- Responsible behaviors teach grown-ups that you can handle more freedom!

- Independent tweens have the confidence and maturity to rely on themselves sometimes and the wisdom to get support when needed.

- Being an independent thinker allows you to have new ideas, creative thoughts, and unique perspectives as well as the opportunity to be a leader!

In this chapter you learned about what it means to be independent, how to get used to taking on more challenges, and that it is okay to ask for help sometimes. So once you have more independence, how do you go about making your own decisions? In the next chapter, you will read about strategies to help you make decisions independently and set goals.

CHAPTER FOUR

GOAL SETTING, TWEEN-STYLE

Imagine that you got invited to a party that takes place the night before your science midterm. Science is your favorite subject and you want to take advanced classes in high school. What do you do? Stay home and study or hang out with your friends? Skipping an extra night of studying might affect your grade, but skipping the party might mean missing out on fun with your friends. How do you decide?

TAKE A MOMENT TO THINK ABOUT THESE STATEMENTS. DO THEY DESCRIBE YOU?

☐ When I am having a tough time making a decision, I can rule out certain choices that I don't want.

☐ I usually think about the consequences before making final decisions.

☐ If my decisions don't work out, I rethink my choices and start again.

☐ I am comfortable asking people I respect for advice.

☐ I make plans for my immediate goals, but also plan for my future.

☐ I set realistic goals for myself.

☐ I make sure that I am calm before making important decisions.

☐ When necessary, I do what I need to do before doing what I want to do.

Sometimes making decisions is really easy. There are many times when decision making is even fun, like trying to come up with a slogan for your school dance. These situations may never lead to stress or worry. But even basic or small decisions can be tough. Sometimes you have too many choices, like when you have to pick one flavor of ice cream out of 25 options.

Decisions can be even more difficult and complicated when they affect your goals. Now that you are a tween, you will get more chances to make decisions and set goals.

Making decisions related to your goals may feel overwhelming at first, but if you break down decisions into small steps, the decision-making process may become more manageable. Having a step-by-step plan can help you to reach your goals more easily. In this chapter, you will learn how to follow a step-by-step process for making decisions and how you can apply this process to setting goals for the future.

DECISIONS, DECISIONS, DECISIONS!

Making decisions can sometimes be time-consuming and even stressful. If you are a human being (and if you are reading this, the answer is obviously "yes!"), then you will probably have to make some difficult decisions in your life. It's not unusual if some of these decisions briefly lead to panic, fear, and a super level of worry. Sometimes even a small decision can cause this big reaction. That's totally understandable. Here are some tips that might help you to feel calm again:

- Clench and unclench your fists, then gently shake them to relax.
- Breathe slowly in through your nose and out through your mouth.
- Realize that usually nothing terrible will happen if either choice is selected. Take a minute to think to yourself, "What's the worst that can happen if I make one choice over the other right now?"
- Go for a quick run, walk, or do another form of exercise you enjoy to burn off the tension.
- Ask a trusted person for an opinion.
- Make your decision, and feel good about it!

Mario's parents offered him several choices for what he could do to celebrate his birthday: a pool party, a paintball party, a laser tag party, or renting out the local pottery studio so he and his friends could create their own pottery.

Mario was confused because he loved all of the choices. His father suggested that he eliminate the choices he liked least. Mario eliminated the pool party because he knew that he could have a few friends over anytime during the summer and spend time in the pool. Slowly, he narrowed down the options until he decided on the laser tag party.

By eliminating choices, do you think Mario found it easier to pick his best option for that particular party?

Do you think this process simplified things for Mario?

Have you ever been faced with a similar problem of having too many options?

How did you make your decision?

---

it's not unusual if some of these decisions briefly lead to panic, fear, and a super level of worry

When making decisions, sometimes you have to think about lots of factors at the same time, such as whether your decision could potentially hurt anyone, whether you are depriving yourself of an experience, and whether your choice will help you to reach your goals for tomorrow.

For example, you might really want to spend the afternoon watching TV, but choose instead to complete an application to try to get into a great summer program, so you can turn it in by the due date.

Thinking through all of these factors can be a tricky thing and hard to get comfortable doing. Here are some tips to help you make decisions:

- Calm yourself. Take a minute to make sure you are relaxed. You may not even feel nervous, but making decisions can cause worry for some kids.

- Think backward. That means thinking about which choice you like the least and then eliminating it. Then keep eliminating choices until you come up with your top choice.

- Think forward. This means trying to figure out the possible consequences of your decisions.

- Rethink decisions. If things don't work out the way you hoped, see if you can re-think your plan and come up with a new direction or path toward your goal.

- Ask for advice. As you already read in this book, even adults ask for help. You may be surprised to know that many teenagers and adults have had similar experiences or decision-making issues and can offer you helpful advice.

TOTAL TWEEN MOMENT: JUAN'S STORY

Juan was offered two tickets to a professional basketball game. The game was at the same time as his friend's beach party. He didn't know what to do. He tried to choose which one he would attend, but he was feeling too frustrated with this decision to pick one.

Juan's older brother told him, "Chill!" Juan immediately started yelling at his brother and said, "Leave me alone. You are being so annoying!" Juan usually doesn't snap at his brother, so he eventually had to admit that he was tense, even though he hadn't realized it.

Have you ever had a similar dilemma?

Have you ever snapped at someone when you were trying to make a decision?

How did it work out?

Probably the most important thing to keep in mind is that life is sometimes written in ink, but usually it is written in pencil. You are allowed to rethink decisions, change your mind, or come up with different plans. Knowing that there is often more than one good choice can help reduce your stress.

asking for help from others shows responsibility and maturity

Say you don't get into a two-week summer theater camp that your friends are attending because the program filled up before you applied. What can you do? If you lock yourself into thinking that this plan was the only way to enjoy your summer, you may end up feeling sad all summer. If you had a back-up plan, you might still end up having a great summer. Maybe there are other two-week summer theater camp sessions. If you attend one of these, your friends may not be there, but you still get to do the activities you love and you may even meet some new friends! Also, if you learned that you need to apply early for things that you want to do, then this experience was useful.

If you get stuck, just ask for advice. Asking for help from others shows responsibility and maturity. Remember, everyone struggles from time to time with making decisions. So you can learn from the experiences of others as they offer you helpful advice!

With calm and careful thinking and some planning, you can make decisions today that help you reach your goals for tomorrow. Now let's talk about how you can set goals for yourself!

SETTING YOUR GOALS

Now that you're a tween with a little more independence to make your own decisions, think about setting some goals for yourself. Not for your parents or friends, but for you. Are there new activities you'd like to try? Things you think you might learn to do better? Maybe you have summer reading and you don't want to wait until the week before school starts to do it. Maybe you want to meet some new kids.

As you think about goals for yourself, there are some things to keep in mind. The first step is to make sure that your goal is realistic and in your control. Unfortunately, as you probably already know, just because you want something, it doesn't mean that you can get it. If you spend the time and energy to make a goal, make sure that it is something that could work out. Trying out for the dance team when you have never taken a dance class might be unrealistic. But trying out for the dance team after you have attended dance camp and practiced routines at home is more doable. As another example, instead of making your goal to be *voted* class president (which is out of your control), a more realistic goal would be to *run* for class president (which is in your control). Setting realistic goals and making a plan to better your chances might mean the difference between reaching a goal and not reaching it. Here are some guidelines for setting realistic goals:

> **if you spend the time and energy to make a goal, make sure that it is something that could work out**

- Be flexible. Consider a back-up plan or smaller goals that you'll be happy with attaining.
- Put in effort. Attention, energy, and time are necessary to reach each small step toward your goal. You have to work to reach your goal.
- Plan. Be sure to have a plan that makes sense to reach your goal.
- Listen. Don't let others discourage you, but listen to their advice.

If your goals are realistic, you are more likely to reach them and have the satisfaction that you accomplished what you set out to do. Aim for the stars you can realistically reach!

After making sure that your goal is realistic and in your control, the next step is to break down the goal into smaller portions. For instance, Jeremy decided that his research project would be to compare different types of governments in different countries. Jeremy had to write a five-page research paper with at least three sources (information from websites or books and articles), and create a PowerPoint presentation for his class.

> **after making sure that your goal is realistic and in your control, the next step is to break down the goal into smaller portions**

Check out how Jeremy divided up his project into 10 steps:

- ▽ Week One

  Step #1: Speak with Ms. Bryant to make sure that I understand the project.

  Step #2: Find several sources relating to my topic. Look for reliable websites and books about my topic.

  Step #3: Write a thesis statement and create an outline of my written report.

- ▷ Week Two

  Step #4: Write a first draft of the introduction and write summaries of the remaining sections. Type up reference sources.

  Step #5: Pick out important points from the report and make a list of what slides to create for the PowerPoint presentation.

  Step #6: Finish the first draft of the report.

- ◁ Week Three

  Step #7: Revise and rewrite the report.

  Step #8: Start making the PowerPoint presentation.

- ▷ Week Four

  Step #9: Complete the PowerPoint presentation.

  Step #10: Review, edit, proofread, and turn in the final report by the deadline.

Learning to break goals down into smaller steps is crucial to success and completion. Planning out the steps may seem like a lot of extra work, but accomplishing each small step builds confidence and keeps you on track to get the job done!

THREE TYPES OF GOALS

There are three different kinds of goals:

- ◁ Immediate goals: things you'd like to accomplish in the next day or two.
- ▷ Short-term goals: stuff you want to work on over the next few months.
- ▽ Long-term goals: big plans or ideas for your future like college or a job.

Just as goals can be accomplished more easily if you break them into smaller steps, long-term goals can sometimes be broken down into immediate and short-term goals. If a long-term goal is to try to get a college scholarship because of your lacrosse skills, your immediate goal might be to improve your skills and your short-term goal might be to make the cut to be on a good lacrosse team. See how this works? Since you may set immediate, short-term, and even long-term goals throughout your entire life, it's important to spend a bit more time reviewing them so you are comfortable with this process.

TOTAL TWEEN MOMENT: **TYLER'S STORY**

Tyler was one of the stars on his Little League team. He was convinced that he would only be happy in life if he became the center fielder for the New York Yankees. He also decided that he didn't have to worry too much about his grades in school because he would get drafted into the Yankee farm club, because of his talent, right after high school. His goal was to be a professional baseball player.

Tyler didn't have to rule out his dream, but needed to have serious back-up plans just in case he didn't make it into the big league. Perhaps Tyler could think about playing for any professional major or minor league team, becoming a baseball coach, or playing baseball just for fun on a neighborhood league.

He also might have wanted to focus more on immediate and short-term goals, such as working on his hitting, catching, and running, and then trying out for the varsity high school team. If that goes well, he could consider college baseball, and hope to later play on any minor or major league team that would consider him.

Does Tyler's story sound familiar?

Are your goals realistic or unrealistic?

What can you do to make them more attainable?

IMMEDIATE GOALS

Immediate goals may sometimes be goals that you can simply achieve very quickly, such as deciding what outfit to wear to the school dance, or making plans for the upcoming weekend. However, they can also be a step toward a larger goal, such as practicing your musical instrument so you can show the band teacher that you have improved and should be considered for a solo in the upcoming concert.

> you may find it helpful to think of your short-term or long-term goals first, and then work backwards

Sarah wanted to be a leader in her school. This was her short-term goal. So she created some immediate goals for the next few days, to help her to begin to take responsibility within the school. Sarah joined the recycling club and asked the peer mentor coach if there was anything that she could do to help younger kids to learn to recycle. Within the next two days, Sarah had attended a club meeting and then read a book in a second grade class the following week. She reached her immediate goals!

Now, take a minute to think of what you really want to happen soon. You may find it helpful to think of your short-term or long-term goals first, and then work backwards to figure out what immediate goals you could accomplish in the next few days.

SHORT-TERM GOALS

Immediate goals can lead to short-term goals. For example, Eva wanted to get into good physical condition so that she had a better chance of getting onto the swim team. Her immediate goal—something she could do in the next few days—was to ask the swim coach and physical education teacher what exercises might build up her strength so she could become a stronger swimmer. Her immediate goal then led her to her short-term goals of practicing these exercises and becoming a better swimmer, getting onto the swim team, and becoming a competitive member of the team.

Other short-term goals could be to get a good grade on a social studies final (the immediate goal might be to study for each quiz that led up to the final) or to get picked for the travel basketball team (the immediate goal might be to have a certain free-throw percentage).

Do you know what your short-term goal might be?

KNOW-HOW NOW:

GET MOTIVATED!

Did you know that there are two different ways to stay motivated to reach your goals? If you really like the goal that you set, such as writing a school spirit song with your best friend, then focusing on the goal can motivate you to get through all the steps you need to do to reach it! However, sometimes you might have goals, such as being prepared to take a final exam, that aren't that exciting to you or that make you worry about whether you will actually reach them. In these situations, focusing on the smaller steps rather than the large goal may decrease worry and stress and get you closer and closer to reaching the goal.

Krause, K., & Freund, A.M. (2014). How to beat procrastination: The role of goal focus. *European Psychologist, 19*(2), 132–144.

LONG-TERM GOALS

Long-term goals are ones that will take a long time to achieve, such as getting into college or getting to be an Eagle Scout in Boy Scouts. Remember to think about breaking down the long-term goal into smaller, more manageable segments and focus on the immediate goals that can lead to the short-term goals, which can lead to the long-term goals. Sound complicated? Let's review all of this.

If you want to eventually be a journalist for a major newspaper, this would be a long-term goal. What can you do today or tomorrow to help you to reach this goal? Your immediate goal might be to join the school newspaper, if your school has one, and begin writing articles as a reporter or trying to start a journalism club at school. You may also try to contact journalists to see if they can offer suggestions for what you can do today to reach your long-term goal. Your short-term goal might be to devote a lot of time to this interest and to writing.

> remember to think about breaking down the long-term goal into smaller, more manageable segments

Not all tweens have long-term goals. Even if you do have long-term goals, you may end up changing them. For instance, when John was setting his long-term goals as a third grader, he said that he wanted to go to Duke University. He loved Duke because they had a great basketball team. However, as a seventh grader, John is thinking more about going to the University of Pennsylvania because his father went there, it has a great business program, and John now hopes to become a successful businessman, like his dad.

Grace's goals show how long-term goals frequently can change from childhood through the tween and teen years. As a three-year-old, she wanted to be a ballerina. At the age of six, Grace decided to become the first woman president of the United States because, she said, "I want everyone to be happy!" By the age of eleven, Grace told her older cousin, "I think I'm going to be an archaeologist because I love learning about ancient Egypt and studying the pyramids."

So, what is your current long-term goal? The only reason to think about this now, even though it may change, is that your immediate and short-term goals may help you to later achieve what you want when you are older.

PRIORITIZING YOUR GOALS

Did you know that people set goals for a bunch of different reasons? For example, there are:

- Goals that you want.
- Goals that you need.
- Goals that you feel you "should" set and reach.

Clearly, having oxygen to breathe is a "need." Going to the beach is a "want," while getting good grades on tests may be a goal you feel is a "should." Some tweens use the phrase "supposed to" in place of "should."

At times, it seems like the "want" is more important than the "should" or even the "need." For example, Nick was excited to go to Africa on a family trip and wanted to get a camera so that he could take pictures. The camera he wanted to get was on sale from 1:00

to 4:00 p.m. on a Wednesday. Nick's mother scheduled him to have some vaccinations that were required for going on this trip at the exact same time as the camera sale. Nick didn't care about the vaccinations that he needed. He cared about getting the camera that he wanted. However, once he realized that without the vaccinations he wouldn't be able to go to Africa and, therefore, wouldn't need the camera, he agreed to what was needed.

Knowing if your goal is a "need," a "want," or a "should" can help you to decide what to pick as your top priority!

MAKING GOALS YOURS

When deciding whether to try something new, it may help to know that many tweens feel proud of themselves for taking on safe, new challenges and pursuing their personal interests and goals.

Being proud of yourself often comes from:

- Doing something that takes effort.
- Doing something that you feel is important.
- Knowing that your decision isn't harmful to you or anyone else.
- Feeling good about the result.

At times, you may feel proud of the actions you are taking, the decision you are making, or the opinions that you are sharing, yet some other people may not agree with you or may even disapprove of your actions or comments. If the people are important in your life, you may want to consider their opinions, although it doesn't necessarily mean you have to change your views or your goals.

If you make choices that you are comfortable with and you are not hurting another individual, then it can be easier to accept the fact that others may sometimes not love what you are doing. For example, Scott decided to take tennis lessons and had no interest in playing soccer, even though most of his friends chose soccer. He felt proud of himself because he made his own decision.

After Maggie's cousin told her about the destruction that a recent hurricane caused to a nearby town, Maggie wanted to do something to help. She talked it over with her parents, and they decided to volunteer, two weekends a month for the next three months, for an organization that gave out food and blankets. Even though Maggie loved hanging out with her friends, she made the decision to devote her time to helping others during this post-hurricane period.

Have you ever made some tough decisions because you felt strongly about doing something or speaking up about something? Did you work hard on your plan for reaching your goals? Even if you didn't reach all of your goals, were you able to feel proud of your efforts?

TWEEN
POINTS

- Decision making is easier if you consider the consequences of each choice.

- Break down long-term goals into manageable steps and make a plan for achieving your goals.

- Make sure that your goals are realistic so that you don't feel frustrated working towards something that isn't possible.

This chapter reviewed immediate, short-term, and long-term goals. You also read about how to figure out if your decision involves a "need," a "want," or a "should" and whether a goal is realistic or unrealistic. Getting to make more of your own decisions and setting goals for yourself is one of the changes you'll likely experience as a tween. In the next chapter, you will read about the physical changes that can happen during the tween years.

CHAPTER FIVE

TWEEN LOOKS AND BODY IMAGE

Since you were an infant, your body has done some miraculous things. You slowly got taller and stronger. Your hair grew without you telling it how to do that. Your heart beats all day and all night. Pretty amazing, when you think about it! Your body will continue to change throughout your life, even though you may not always notice the changes from one day to the next.

☐ I am comfortable with the physical changes that are happening to me.

☐ I am comfortable talking with my parents about how my body is changing.

☐ I have a realistic and healthy idea of how my body should look.

☐ I like my body as it is!

☐ I have a tween style now that fits my personality— and my parents approve!

☐ My body language shows that I am confident in who I am.

☐ I keep myself clean and showered without being reminded by my parents.

Now that you are a tween, the changes may feel dramatic. The tween years are not just about waiting to become a teenager. Your body is changing. Your look is changing. You are entering puberty. Such dramatic changes leave some tweens happy while other tweens are embarrassed or uncomfortable. Some tweens are happy and embarrassed at the same time. What about you?

In this chapter, you will read more about the physical changes in your body that happen during puberty and what a healthy body image and tween style feels like.

DEALING WITH PUBERTY AND SUDDENLY LOOKING DIFFERENT

When you enter the tween years, your body may go through growth spurts and changes quickly and in new ways. You may all of a sudden grow taller than your friends or you may notice that your friends are growing while you remain the same height. This time of change can last all the way through your late teens or into your early 20s. One day you might look like your old self, and the next day you might notice some differences and even think, "Wow! How did this happen? Why did I suddenly change?"

In addition to your appearance, your body is changing on the inside. Generally speaking, puberty is the time when your body gets ready to be an adult. Your body begins to mature into an adult body that is capable of sexual reproduction—that is, able to make a baby. All this happens because hormones (chemicals in your body) signal your body to grow and mature. Lots of body parts can start to change: your brain, bones, muscles, skin, hair, and chest, as well as your sex organs—penis and scrotum if you are a boy, and ovaries, uterus, and vagina if you are a girl. Sex organs, both inside and outside of your body, are generally considered to be very private parts of a person. That might be why talking about puberty can make some people feel uncomfortable! All this change can be confusing or overwhelming to some tweens.

> in addition to your appearance, your body is changing on the inside

You may have already learned about the physical changes you will be (or are) facing. Many schools have human development or health education classes where teachers talk about the specifics of puberty, how your body is maturing, and how human reproduction works (how babies are made). You may get a lot of useful information at school, but it is important to talk with your parents about what is happening, too, so they can explain it and talk with you about how puberty is affecting you.

Sometimes parents don't exactly know when or how to talk about these changes with you, and you might feel uncomfortable bringing it up yourself. Here are some conversation-starters that might help you to talk with your parents about puberty:

- "Can I talk to you privately about my body changing?"
- "When you were my age, did your body do things that made you embarrassed?"
- "When you were my age, how did you handle the changes I'm going through?"

Your parents might need time to prepare for this discussion, so ask first if they can set aside time for this conversation. Chelsea and her mom ordered pizza one day when they were alone at home, and they talked. Her mom also gave her a book about puberty and the changes that occur during this time in a tween's life. They read it and then discussed it together. Think about what you want to talk about with your parent and when you might be able to have this talk.

it's okay to say that you're not comfortable talking about this topic right now

There may be a time when your parent comes to you and wants to talk about puberty. If you are uncomfortable, it's okay to say that you're not comfortable talking about this topic right now. But still try to have the discussion soon. Some tweens may be tempted to say, "I got it covered. I already learned all about this from school and my friends." Remember, though, that it helps to have an adult know what you are thinking, to educate you on what is happening and what will happen, and to be a support for you.

Boys and girls go through many of the same physical, mental, and emotional changes, but there are some changes that are unique to just boys or to just girls. You may have studied human reproduction and puberty in school, or you may have already talked to your parents about it. So let's just briefly review how puberty and development can make a tween feel.

BECOMING A TWEEN BOY

People usually notice when a tween boy's voice starts changing into a deeper adult voice. Some boys become very self-conscious if their voice "cracks" or if it sounds raspy while it changes. If you are a boy, has this happened to you or others you know? How do you feel about it? How do you handle this situation and your feelings about it?

First, it's a natural change that will end when you get older. Eventually your voice will become deeper and more adult-like, and everyone will forget if it cracked or squeaked. In the meantime, how you react to it and how you respond to others who might comment can make a big difference. You might be okay with your changing voice sometimes. Or, you may feel super embarrassed and annoyed by it at other times. Everyone reacts in their own personal way. Keith's voice cracked when he was doing a solo during chorus class. At first he was embarrassed until his friend whispered to him, "Mine does that too. Not a big deal. Just tell them that you are putting your unique accent on the music." Keith did that, with a smile on his face. He was surprised that his classmates laughed with him, not at him! Like Keith, you might need to just roll with it sometimes.

As boys get older, they begin growing more hair on their bodies, faces, chests, underarms, and pubic (also called the private) areas. Usually hair first starts to grow around the base of a boy's penis and around his pubic area, and then appears on other parts of his body—his upper lip, armpits, and chest. For some boys, growing hair may be a proud moment. They are happy about the changes! For them, it is a welcome sign of confidence and maturity, and shows that they are growing up. Evan noticed "mustache hairs" and told his friends, "I guess I'm more mature than you. I'm already growing a mustache!" Evan wasn't trying to hurt his friends; he was trying to point out that growing older is an exciting process and he was looking forward to the adventure. Other tween boys, however, are upset by this sign of growing up. Maybe they aren't ready for the change or are uncomfortable with the attention. Maybe all of these physical changes are too much too soon for them! It's normal to be excited about growing hair, but it's also normal to feel uncomfortable about it.

If you're a boy, how do you feel about your height? Are you getting taller? Have you noticed your body shape is changing? Maybe your shoulders are getting broader, you build muscles more easily, and your arms and legs suddenly seem to get longer. Do you worry about developing normally, or wonder if you will ever be tall or look physically strong? Lots of boys talk about how they feel about their height and whether or not they have muscles. Some tweens are busy comparing themselves to others and get nervous if they are shorter, taller, or have smaller muscles than the other boys in their grade.

Did you know that lots of tween boys are shorter than girls at this stage? If you lined up everyone in your class, you would see a lot of variety in height! Everyone grows at a different rate, so there really isn't a normal or abnormal height for all tweens. Over time, you'll grow to the height you'll be as an adult. Your doctor can certainly tell you if there is any concern about your growth rate, but usually it's just a matter of being patient. Remember that you can walk tall, even if you aren't the tallest kid in your class.

> while a lot of physical changes occur in the tween and teen years, these changes don't define you

Boys will also eventually notice changes to their sex organs. A boy's penis will get larger and his scrotum and the testicles inside will lower. With these changes, you may also notice that your body reacts in ways that it might not have before puberty, both when you are awake and when you are asleep. Your penis may become tight (longer and wider) and stand upright more often. This is called an erection. Erections are normal physical reactions to emotions, thoughts, or even sensations such as touch. Some boys are so worried about this that they talk to their parents about buying certain clothing that might allow them to hide any spontaneous erections. If you now feel embarrassed when you get an erection, keep in mind that sometimes these spontaneous erections just happen, and you can just wait until the penis relaxes again.

While a lot of physical changes occur in the tween and teen years, these changes don't define you. Height and body build are only physical characteristics, not who you are. Plus you have no control over the changes that happen inside of you. All together, these changes do not determine your personality or how successful you will be.

Can you feel confident in who you are even if you aren't totally comfortable with how you look right now? While you actually do have some control over your looks—such as how you dress, or whether you comb your hair—you have a lot of control over who you are and how you live your life.

TOTAL TWEEN MOMENT: MARK'S & DERRICK'S STORY

Mark's mom and dad were both tall. Even though Mark was smaller than some of his friends, at the age of eight, his doctor let him know that he will most likely have a growth spurt in his teenage years. Mark is now nineteen and is 6'1" and taller than almost all of his other friends. His genetics played an important role in this physical characteristic.

On the other hand, Derrick's parents were not tall. Derrick ended up being 5'6". Derrick said, "I'm fine. Being taller doesn't mean anything unless I let it. I want to be an engineer and I never heard that being tall was a requirement! I know my friends like me, too, so my height doesn't matter." Derrick appeared to be confident and didn't seem intimidated by taller kids. Because of this, his mother described him as walking tall. If Derrick was embarrassed or upset about his height and jealous of his taller friends, this could have affected his behavior and attitude. Have you thought about your height like this?

Does Derrick have a positive attitude about his size?

How would you feel if you were shorter or taller than your friends?

BECOMING A TWEEN GIRL

During the tween and teen years, girls develop breasts and their hips round out. A girl's body will often start to now develop into a shape that is more curvy and full like an adult woman. These changes can make some girls feel proud and happy. Other girls may feel uncomfortable or even embarrassed. Maybe they aren't ready for their bodies to develop this way and maybe it is happening too soon for them. Many girls prefer to keep these changes a bit more private at first until they get used to what's happening. Like boys, girls may ask their parents to buy them clothing that allows for more privacy, like less form-fitting tops or sports bras. It can be uncomfortable to be the first kid in your class to be visibly going through puberty! Some girls, on the other hand, want clothing that shows off these changes, like tighter tops or short skirts, and this sometimes leads to parent-child disagreements or discussions about the appropriate clothing for the tween years.

Just like boys, girls start growing hair on their pubic area (on their lower abdomen just above where their legs come together). Girls may also notice more hair on their legs, arms, and armpits. If you are a girl, you may start wondering if you should shave the hair on your legs or underarms. If you are thinking about shaving your legs or armpits, talk about it with your parents.

As you just read, a boy's voice begins to change and get deeper as he moves closer to the teen years. Did you know that girls' voices may change a little as they get older, too? It's often not as noticeable, but you may notice a subtle difference in your voice or the voice of a girl that you know. It's a natural change that occurs during puberty.

TOTAL TWEEN MOMENT: CARLA'S STORY

Carla was embarrassed to wear a bra to school. She worried about being treated differently by the boys and she thought other girls would wonder why she needs a bra when they don't. She seemed to be entering puberty before most of her friends. She didn't want to be different.

When Carla returned home from school after wearing her bra to school for the first time, she told her mother, "I know one boy noticed but didn't say anything. Alexa asked me how it feels, but that was okay because we're friends and talk about everything. I'm glad this first day is over. I think I made a big deal over it and it really isn't a big deal."

Has a situation like this happened to you or someone you know?

How do you think Carla felt about how she handled this experience?

What would you do?

How would you feel if you were Carla going to school wearing a bra for the first time?

In addition to the physical changes on the outside, other changes are happening inside a girl's body. Beginning in puberty, a girl's body starts to mature so that eventually it will become capable of sexual reproduction (able to make a baby). Hormones (chemicals in your body) will signal your ovaries and uterus to develop and mature. During the tween years, you may start to menstruate, also commonly described as getting your period. Many girls get their period when they are between 11 and 13 years old, but a lot of girls get it earlier or later. There is no exact age when you are supposed to get your period. During your menstrual cycle, the lining of your uterus thickens with blood and tissue, making your uterus the perfect place to grow and nourish a baby during pregnancy. Your body makes this lining every month. If you are not pregnant, the lining isn't needed, and it is discharged through your vagina. This is your "period." Your period typically lasts a few days to a week, and occurs about once a month.

talk to your parents—they can help you to get ready and to feel comfortable with this natural change in your life

To absorb this menstrual flow, girls wear pads or tampons made of soft material. Used pads or tampons are thrown away when they are full. During your period, you may have cramps, you might feel extra emotional, or you might have pimples or swollen breasts. All girls are different, so some (or all) of these things may not happen to you. If you do experience these symptoms, they are temporary, but they can make you feel uncomfortable or tired.

Girls have lots of different reactions to getting their period. Olivia was embarrassed. Mary was super proud and excited. Brooke felt inconvenienced by it. Some girls worry that kids will tease them. Other girls are worried that they will have their period at school or at camp, so they keep a pad with them in their backpack or locker. You might have other reactions or mixed reactions. If your friend gets her period before you, how would you feel? If you get yours first, how would you deal with this? Talk to your parents—they can help you to get ready and to feel comfortable with this natural change in your life.

EVERYONE CHANGES!

As you just read, both boys and girls face changes in their bodies during the tween and teen years. So, if you feel self-conscious or uncomfortable with the changes you are experiencing, you might want to ask yourself, "Why am I uncomfortable? I know everyone has gone through or will go through these changes." Do you have an answer for this question? In addition, it may be helpful to think about the following:

- It's okay to change at a different pace than your friends. Everyone eventually becomes an adult with an adult body.

- Everyone's body changes; it's natural.

- If you feel embarrassed by the physical changes you go through, remind yourself that they are natural.

- If kids tease you, politely remind them that they will also change.

- Your body won't change into an adult's body overnight, and it may take time for you to get used to the changes. Just try to be patient as you grow through your tween and teen years.

Remember, the changes you are experiencing are natural, and everyone goes through them at some point!

LIKING YOUR BODY

Body image is how you see yourself, not how others see you or how you really are. You may want to take a few minutes to *really* look at yourself in the mirror. Look at your hair, your eyes, your nose, your mouth, your cheeks, your ears, and so forth. Then look at your entire face—all the parts together. Can you find reasons to feel positively about how you look? Do you like what you see? Did you know that if you feel confident about how you look, it's likely that others will find you more attractive?

Some tweens want to be as handsome or as beautiful as the models, movie stars, and athletes they see in magazines. Did you know that magazines sometimes modify photos to change body sizes and hide imperfections and make celebrities seem even more slim and attractive than they really are? If you want to be like the people you see in the magazines, you may be competing with an impossible image that may have been changed and "improved" through the assistance of production staff and technology.

As a tween, you may feel a little awkward as your body changes. While you adjust to your maturing body, you may find that you are overly critical of how you look. You may find that you judge yourself more harshly than you would ever judge a friend. If you tend to look for the negative, try to change your focus. Look at what you like about your body and remember that your personality, and how you act and react to others, are the keys to making and keeping friends—not your weight, height, or other physical factors!

Chloe was unhappy with her body. She started feeling upset about "being fat." Her parents did not feel that she was overweight and her pediatrician said she was fine. Yet, Chloe always felt that she needed to lose weight. So Chloe began exercising for hours each night and not eating much. Eventually, her body image concerns and her exercise and dieting were so extreme that she ended up passing out one day and was hospitalized. She was diagnosed with anorexia nervosa. Most kids won't get to this dangerous point, but many will see themselves as too fat, too thin, or want to change other parts of their face or body.

KNOW-HOW NOW:

THE PERFECT BODY?

Did you know that some teens believe that their life would be better and they would be happier if they had a perfect body? In a study of teens in America and in France, researchers found that almost 75% of American teens "believe that they would be much happier and find life easier if they had a flawless body" compared to less than 25% of the French teens. Does this surprise you? Why do you think that U.S. teens believed this more than the French teens? Do you agree that your life would be better if you had the perfect body? Do you think there is such a thing as a perfect body? Can you accept your body as it is?

Ferron, C. (1997). Body image in adolescence: Cross-cultural research—Results of the preliminary phase of a quantitative survey. *Adolescence, 32,* 735–745.

Some tweens have even wanted to stay home from school because they found a pimple on their face. If you think about it, a pimple is a small thing and a very small percentage of your body! When Douglas got a pimple, however, it was all he focused on. He explained,

"All I see is the zit. It's like it has power to make me focus just on it. I'm afraid kids will stare at it all day if I go to school." Do you agree with Douglas? If so, remember that you are still you, whether you have a pimple or not. If you try to put your hand over it all day, it may only make others curious about it. Also, if you don't make a big deal about it, often others won't either. If you get pimples often, though, you may want to ask your parents if you should see your doctor to decide if you need some medicine to treat them.

> you don't have to work to be just like another person

The good news is that you are unique. The bad news, at times, is that you *feel* unique, and you don't want to be different from your friends. If you focus on being different and maybe feel less capable or less attractive or more insecure than others, then being unique could seem like a negative. Many tweens have days when they feel insecure or less together than their friends. However, there really is good news about being unique! You don't have to work to be just like another person. You can learn to appreciate the fact that no one is exactly like you on the inside or outside. Even if you have an identical twin, there are still differences of which you are probably aware. It may be helpful to think about the following:

- Your body image is how you think about your body, not necessarily how your body really is.
- It's important to consider whether your body image is realistic.
- If you are not happy with your body image, ask your parents to see if your image is accurate, and, if you generally trust them, trust what they say!
- If you do have some realistic concerns—such as concerns regarding your weight, or wanting to build muscles—ask your doctor for safe suggestions.

One thing is definite: your body will change throughout your lifetime. If you learn to accept yourself now, you can enjoy life without focusing too much on things you may not be able to change. Also, you can take control of trying to change things that realistically might make you healthier, such as eating healthy and exercising.

LET'S TALK ABOUT (SIGH...) HYGIENE

While many tweens roll their eyes and feel annoyed or embarrassed when adults talk to them about hygiene or cleanliness, try not to skip reading this section. It's short, and it might allow you to think more about your hygiene choices, such as showering, having clean hands and nails, brushing your hair and teeth, and wearing clothes that aren't dirty or wrinkled.

As a tween, your body is making all sorts of hormones. This means that you may start to have a body odor if you sweat a lot and don't shower. Did you know that other kids may smell your body odor, even if you don't recognize it because you are always around yourself and your personal smells? Bad breath may also now be noticed in a new way, but that is usually easily cured with the help of a toothbrush and toothpaste. Whether you have wax hanging around the outside of your ears, whether you wipe your nose with your sleeve, whether you have food from breakfast still on your mouth, and whether you have recently washed your hair are all things that tweens begin to notice.

once you get into a routine, it shouldn't take more than 15 minutes each day

Leah was always busy with sports and getting good grades. One day, though, she came home crying. Eventually, she told her mother, "I was so embarrassed today because Brian asked me to move away from him in the cafeteria. He said I smelled like I must have hugged a skunk. I was always just too busy to do the showering thing. It takes so much time to do my ears, my hair, and everything else. I'm going to do it now, though."

Brian certainly wasn't polite! But he did voice an observation that others probably thought, but didn't say, because they liked Leah too much to hurt her feelings. Leah and her mom worked out a showering schedule that fit with all of her other activities.

Knowing that tweens are very aware of their own and others' bodies, it's time to consider paying special attention to how you care for your body. Once you get into a routine, it shouldn't take more than 15 minutes each day.

PRESENTING...YOU!

Every time you walk into a room with other people, you are sharing information about yourself. Other people may not be judging whether you are good or bad or attractive or not, but they are learning something about you. They may quickly pick up cues as to whether you are outgoing, upbeat, and smiling. In this section, you will have a chance to think about how you present yourself to the world.

There are many things that boys and girls communicate through both their choice of style and through their behaviors. Here are a few things to think about:

- What message will other kids get from how you present yourself?

- Is the message one you want them to get?

- There is an old saying, "When people walk into a room, they are judged by their looks. When they leave, they are judged by their wits." So, even though your physical presentation and style matters for first impressions, your personality and ideas may matter even more. In other words, your personality is what may be remembered more than your looks!

- There is another old saying, "You can't always tell a book by its cover." So, if you want to help others out, try to make your outside style match who you are on the inside. For example, sometimes t-shirts have slogans that can show that you are interested in certain kinds of videos or sports. This might be a clue to who you are and your interests, thoughts, or personality.

- If you find that you have to hide your style from your parents—for example, by changing your clothes when you get to school—think about why your parents don't like your style and whether you may want to change it. Your parents may seem old-fashioned, but they may have had a different style from their own parents, too. Try explaining your style to your parents and they may understand more about you and your choices.

- Decide if you are picking a style just to be accepted by other kids, even though it makes you uncomfortable. If this is true, and the other kids really won't accept you if you don't have their same style, are they real friends?

Before reading more, take a minute to think about who you are and how you can help others to understand you by how you act and look. Remember that your choice of clothing, your hygiene and grooming, your behavior, your sense of humor, your interests, and even whether you are a good listener are all key ways that others can learn about you.

CARRYING YOURSELF WITH CONFIDENCE

Style is not just about the clothes you wear; it's also about your attitude and how you carry yourself. Did you know that identical twins can appear very different to a stranger, just because of how they walk and talk and communicate with their body language?

Take a few moments to think about your own confidence level and how you show it to others. Here are some questions to think about:

- Do you try to hide even while you are standing next to other kids?
- Do you believe that others will reject you if they really get to know you?
- Are you comfortable sharing your ideas?
- Are you comfortable admitting when you don't know something?
- Can you easily list three reasons why you are likeable and others should enjoy getting to know you?

As you probably realize, if you answered "yes" to either of the first two items above, you may not be as confident as you might want. If you answered "yes" to any of the last three items above, you're on the right track for becoming confident!

Here are some tips to help you to confidently survive all of the changes of tween-hood:

- If you are teased because of your changing appearance, act confident and just say, "Whatever," or "So, what?" or "Grow up!"
- Have a support team of people you trust to talk to, so you don't feel alone.
- Focus on changes you feel positive about to build confidence.

Every tween is changing, even though you may not always know how other kids are dealing with it. It may take time to feel comfortable with who you are and to become confident. Remember that you can focus a lot on the negative and feel down or focus more on your abilities and other positive characteristics and feel better. Also, remember, you don't have to go through this journey alone.

TWEEN POINTS

- Feeling confident can actually make you **look** different!

- Pick your style for you, not because of your friends.

- While you may feel alone while you go through the changes of your tween years, all kids go through them at some point.

In this chapter, you read all about how to feel more comfortable and confident with your changing body and how to talk with supportive adults about these changes. Developing your tween style, taking care of your body, and communicating confidence through body language were also reviewed. Now that you have spent time thinking about how you physically present yourself to the world, it's time to explore how you might feel about others. In the next chapter, you will read about crushes, flirting, and dating.

CHAPTER SIX

CRUSHES, FLIRTING, AND DATING

Puberty doesn't only change how your body looks. It also can change how you feel about boys and girls. During the tween years, you might experience your first crush, you might feel attracted to someone, or you might want to have a boyfriend or girlfriend. Or not!

TAKE A MOMENT TO THINK ABOUT THE ITEMS LISTED BELOW. DO ANY OF THEM DESCRIBE YOU?

☐ I am comfortable feeling attracted to someone.

☐ I am comfortable not having crushes right now.

☐ If I have romantic feelings for someone and I know that he or she doesn't feel the same way, I always try to be respectful.

☐ I think about the consequences before I decide to flirt with someone.

☐ I don't date or flirt just because I feel pressured to do so by my friends.

☐ I know how to handle teasing from others if they learn about my feelings for someone.

☐ I know how to respectfully tell someone else that I'm flattered but not interested in dating him or her.

Remember reading that it's okay to be on your own timeline during the tween years? Well, this definitely applies to crushes, flirting, and dating. Throughout the rest of this chapter, you will read more about how you might feel, act, and react when romantic feelings happen to you or to others. You'll also read about crushes, flirting, dating, fooling around, and learn that if you don't have any of these feelings, that's fine, too!

FEELING ATTRACTED TO OTHERS

During the tween years, you might experience your first crush on someone. Having a crush means you have romantic or sexual feelings toward someone else whom you consider special. Are you experiencing your first serious crush or feelings of attraction for another person?

Did you know that people are attracted to others for many reasons, and one person's crush may feel different than another person's? Feeling attracted to someone is difficult to explain—sometimes the feelings are very strong. Sometimes you just kind of "know it" and feel attracted to someone. Sometimes just seeing that person or hearing his or her voice can make you excited and happy. Sometimes your emotions are all in a whirl and you feel nervous or embarrassed. Maybe you have tremendous affection for that person. Maybe you want to spend time hanging out with that person or maybe you imagine having a loving romance with that person. You may feel physically attracted to that person, too. Patrick liked Jenny because she was athletic and competitive, looked "cute" and had "great eyes." Lara had a crush on Peter because he "has muscles, is tall, is kind, and is smart." Charlie was interested in Gabe because he loved his laugh and liked how serious he was about his school grades.

As you probably know, some girls are attracted to boys and others are attracted to girls. Some boys may be attracted to girls, while others are interested in boys. Feeling attracted to someone can feel exciting and wonderful, complicated and confusing, or like a combination of reactions. Even though many people end up with a partner of the opposite sex, others end up with partners of the same sex. Whether you feel attracted to boys or girls (or both), your attraction just happens naturally. For now, just keep in mind that you can take your time to figure out who you are attracted to. The tween years are a time of discovery and a time of change. There is no need to try to understand yourself and your feelings all at once.

Did you know that it's not unusual for tweens to have crushes on people they have never met? Is this normal? Absolutely! It gives tweens a chance to explore their feelings, yet have the safety of not having to sit near that person every day in class. Feelings are never wrong or bad. Feeling attracted to someone is perfectly natural. But if you end up obsessed and constantly thinking about the person, you are not focusing on school, responsibilities, or friends, and you find that you have a crush on someone who is unlikely to return your feelings, then your crush has become a concern. If this happens, take a step back and remind yourself that if your crush is impacting your life in a not-so-good way, it's time to move on!

> Feelings are never wrong or bad. Feeling attracted to someone is perfectly natural

Even if the kid you are attracted to is in your school or in your class, you can still just privately enjoy your feelings. When Shari was hanging out with Terri, she told Terri about her crush on Michael. Terri offered to talk to Michael for her and tell him about Shari's crush on him. Terri thought it would be good to find out if Michael liked Shari too. But Shari immediately said, "No! Don't! I'd just die from embarrassment if you told him." Do you understand Shari's reaction?

When you have a crush on someone, it's okay to want to keep it private. Take some time to just enjoy the experience. Later, you can think about whether to share your feelings with the person you are attracted to, or even whether you should share them with friends.

Think about these questions before deciding whether to share your feelings with friends or with the person you have a crush on:

- Is it possible that your friends will tease you or the person that you like?
- Is your crush constant? Or do your feelings switch on and off?
- Is it possible that other kids or your crush will want to talk about dating?
- Are you comfortable with your feelings not being private?
- Is it possible that you may be judged by others in a way that you don't want if you do share your feelings?

Now, let's say that you learn that another kid has a crush on you, and you don't have a crush on that kid. What should you do? You really don't have to do anything. But remember that you don't want to flirt with the other person and mislead him or her, laugh about his or her feelings with others, or ask the other person for favors because you know he or she likes you.

If you feel that crushes, flirting, and dating are new and even stressful, just remember to take your time! Ask questions! And get advice! It's important to know that you don't have to figure this out all at once or on your own. Get a support team—this may include your friends, parents, and other trusted adults—that can help you to understand yourself, accept yourself, and figure out what you can do with your new and changing feelings.

TOTAL TWEEN MOMENT: KELLY'S STORY

Kelly and Justin had been close friends since pre-school and she didn't think of him as a boyfriend. However, one day, when Justin and Kelly were watching a TV show where two high school kids were dating, Justin said, "Maybe that will be us in high school!"

Later that evening, Kelly talked about Justin with her two older sisters. She asked them, "Why would he think like that? We're just friends!" Kelly's sisters said she can't program Justin to think or feel in a certain way and she needs to be careful not to hurt his feelings.

The next day, Kelly said, "Justin, I'm not even thinking about dating right now. I really like being super close friends. Let's stay like this."

Kelly couldn't wait to tell her sisters how Justin replied. Kelly said, "I talked to Justin and told him I'm not ready to date. And guess what? Justin told me he was getting nervous around me and that he was relieved that I want to stay close and keep the friendship. I think we're cool."

What do you think of how Kelly handled this situation?

Have you ever been in a similar situation?

DEALING WITH TEASING OR FLIRTING

Did you know that sometimes girls and boys tease the kids that they like, even though it makes the other person feel uncomfortable? Sound confusing? It does tend to confuse a lot of tweens! Many tweens begin to look at other tweens in a different way ("She's hot!" "He's cute!"). You may feel uncomfortable or uncertain about how to approach a kid you are interested in. Sometimes, tweens use teasing, which can be hurtful, as a way to connect to someone without dealing with the new feelings directly.

> tweens may use teasing, which can be hurtful, as a way to connect to someone without dealing with the new feelings directly

Arthur thought that Isabelle was really cute and he wanted to talk to her. Every time he got close to her, though, he became shy and just kept noticing how cute she was. He was embarrassed and found that he was much more comfortable being around her if he was teasing her. He didn't want to hurt her feelings, but he didn't want it to seem like he really liked her. Unfortunately, Isabelle's feelings got hurt, her friends got mad at Arthur, and Arthur made even more jokes because, as he said, "I didn't know what else to do."

If you are nervous being around a person you are attracted to, here are some things that might work for you and not hurt the other person's feelings:

- Just say "hi." It's a simple word but it lets the person know you are there.
- Ask how the person's weekend went.
- Compliment the person on a project or a comment he or she made in class.
- Join an activity that you might enjoy and that the person might be involved in too, so you can talk about the activity.

But what if you are the tween being teased? You can't be totally sure why the other person is teasing you. Maybe it's because the person has a crush on you and doesn't know how to handle it. Or maybe the kid just likes picking on you to make you uncomfortable. Later in this book, you will read more about how to handle the second kind of teasing.

But for a minute, let's figure out some steps you can take if you think the person is teasing you because he or she is attracted to you, like Arthur did to Isabelle. Here are some strategies you can try:

- Say that the teasing has hurt your feelings, and you know that he is usually nice, so you are confused. This can encourage the person to share respectful and positive words with you.

- Start a conversation with him about a topic you both feel comfortable talking about.

- Walk away if you feel disrespected. No matter what the person's reasons for teasing you are, you don't need to accept being treated like this.

- Remember not to tease back. You know how hurtful it can be.

- Seek out an adult for support and guidance.

Like teasing, flirting is also used to get the attention of your crush. When you flirt you are acting on your feelings and letting the person know that you enjoy being together, or that you are attracted to him or her. You may laugh a lot at jokes, be extra supportive of that person, or spend a lot of time around the person.

It's okay to flirt and still not want to date, if it doesn't make the other person uncomfortable or mislead the person into thinking that you want to date. William had a crush on Melanie. At the age of twelve, he didn't want to actually date or have anyone say he has a girlfriend. He did want to let Melanie know that he liked her, though. He started hanging around her a lot. He texted her for help with homework, because he wanted to connect with her. He often found himself looking at her when she was nearby. What do you think could happen next? Here are some possible outcomes to William's behavior:

- Melanie is flattered by the attention, but glad William didn't ask her out.
- Melanie is flattered by the attention, but confused as to why William didn't ask her out.
- Melanie's or William's friends tease them about liking each other, thus making both of them uncomfortable.
- Other tweens may consider Melanie or William "taken" because everyone believes they are dating each other already.

If you decide that you want to flirt, always remember the other person's feelings, how your friends and other kids might react, and whether you are flirting due to peer pressure or because it feels right to you. Peer pressure can be powerful. It means that friends or other kids are pressuring you to act or think in a certain way. If they pressure you to do something that you want to do anyway, it may not even feel like pressure. However, if they pressure you to do things that you don't feel are right or don't feel comfortable doing right now, then it can sometimes be very stressful.

> if you aren't interested in a particular person, it's sometimes better to just respectfully and carefully explain this

If friends decide that you (or all of you) should flirt with other people, but you really don't want to, put on the brakes before reacting. As you probably already know, flirting is about sharing your feelings of attraction with another person, so both your feelings *and* the feelings of the other person should always be considered. It's sometimes hard to resist peer pressure, though. If you aren't sure how to handle this, ask for advice from your parents, other trusted adults, or even older siblings.

Now, let's say someone is flirting with you and you aren't attracted to that person. What can you do?

It's okay to let the person flirting with you know that you are flattered by the attention, but you just want to be friends right now, or that you aren't ready to date anyone. However, if you end up dating another tween a week later, then your original admirer might feel that you were dishonest and end up with hurt feelings.

If you aren't interested in a particular person, it's sometimes better to just respectfully and carefully explain this to the other person. You could say something like, "You're really nice and someone else would love to flirt with or even date you. It's hard for me to say this, but I'm not that person. I'm really sorry if I hurt your feelings." This way, you aren't leaving the other person feeling that no one will ever like him or her, and you communicate your interest in *not* being hurtful but in being honest.

DATING...OR NOT

Some tweens enjoy feeling attracted to another person and want to do more than flirt. They may want to date or "go out." Kids sometimes use the word "date" to mean that two tweens declare their attraction for each other, maybe talk or text a lot, and sometimes may go places together, or even hold hands. Tween dating generally means that you are exclusive and that you may call that person your boyfriend or girlfriend.

Keep in mind you can't date someone without that person's agreement. Both kids have to agree that they are dating. So before telling your friends that you are involved in a relationship and dating someone, make sure that the other person knows and agrees! Alison told her friends that she and David were dating. Eventually, one of David's friends asked David about this. He said, "I didn't know that!" David wasn't happy about Alison telling everyone that he was her boyfriend and they were dating.

Now, imagine that David and Alison both decided that they wanted to date. It can be helpful to spend time figuring out:

- What does this really mean to them and what will others think?
- What will they both do in this relationship?
- What are the limits of this dating relationship?

Setting ground rules can help avoid misunderstandings later. Ciaran and Yana talked and both wanted to date each other. Yana said, "I can't actually go places with you. My parents won't allow that. And, none of the sexual stuff. Okay?" Ciaran totally agreed with Yana. They started dating based on their mutually agreed upon definition of dating. If you find that you and the other person have very different ideas of what dating should be, maybe it's not the right time for both of you to date. Dating is not supposed to make either person uncomfortable!

Dating can be complicated, so it's always helpful to speak with your parents about how to navigate this new time in your life. Also, check with your parents to see if they agree that it is okay for you to date right now. You can also talk about how to make sure that you only move forward at a pace that is comfortable to you and that you are respectful of the other person. Never try to pressure someone or guilt someone into dating you. In addition, it's helpful to discuss whether dating will possibly hurt your reputation because others may think you are moving fast sexually or are not interested in just being part of a social group right now.

When thinking about dating, the idea of breaking up isn't on a lot of people's minds. However, think about it before dating. What will happen if you both or only one of you decides you don't want to date anymore? If you think breaking up will permanently mess up your friendship with this person or hurt some of your other friendships (will friends have to take sides?), it may not be time to start thinking about dating.

FOOLING AROUND?

There are some kids who love the idea of being in love and dating, and look forward to fooling around with their boyfriend or girlfriend. This means that they want to start kissing or touching another person in a sexual way. These kids are experiencing a lot of new things all at once. Did you know that even these kids may sometimes feel unsure about whether they are ready? If you are thinking about dating and being sexual with your boyfriend or girlfriend, it can be extremely helpful to take your time, make sure you don't do anything because of peer pressure, and talk with your parents and other trusted people in your life to discuss the possible consequences of taking these actions.

It's also super important to listen to the wishes of the other tween. Here are some things to remember:

- Take your time—growing up and dating is a journey, not a race!
- Romance and fooling around are very personal and should not be influenced by peer pressure.
- Make sure that you and your partner are both comfortable with whatever you decide to do.
- Talk to your parents to make sure this is the right time for you to get involved in dating and romance.

Some tweens like the idea of flirting but really don't want to be anyone's boyfriend or girlfriend right now, so you can't assume just by another person's behavior that you know what they want. You probably already know that if you want to fool around and the other person is uncomfortable with that, this is not a time to try to convince that person. You cannot force someone to do something they don't want to do! So instead, prepare for rejection—not of you as a person, but of your suggestion—and find a way to be okay with that (having a support team can help!). Many tweens are focused on their own changing body, feelings, expectations, thoughts, and crushes, and aren't really interested in dating or fooling around right now. You have to respect that.

There are kids who hint that they are fooling around, but actually they are simply just talking or texting a lot with the other person. They may say they are doing something different so that other tweens will think that they are cool or grown-up. Or rumors may be spread that they are fooling around, even when they are not and are just close friends.

HANGING WITH GROUPS

Many tweens enjoy talking with and hanging out with groups of kids. It gives them the chance to feel included, to get to know lots of kids, and enjoy the friendship of many different kinds of kids. Remember that you don't have to totally leave your childhood friends, interests, and activities behind. It's okay to have old friends or new friends, and it's okay to play board games together, go bowling, go to the movies, or play videogames together. It's a great way to ease into the transition to being a teen. It is perfectly fine to be a tween who wants nothing to do with dating. Many, many tweens are focused on their activities and their friends. Since there is plenty of time later to date, there is no reason to rush into the teenage years before you are ready.

Some tweens say that they like thinking about dating, but want to get to know the kids they are attracted to better and just become friends with them. After all, puberty can sometimes add some new qualities to even old friendships, so getting to hang out as tweens may be different than when you were hanging out as seven-year-olds.

As you may recall from Chapter One, Emma and Harry were not interested in dating yet, but Andrew was. There is no one right way to feel. Sometimes kids act like they want to date because of peer pressure, or because they don't want to be seen as

it is perfectly fine to be a tween who wants nothing to do with dating different. It takes some courage to do what feels right, even if some kids might lead you to believe that "everyone is dating."

Any choice you make about how to handle flirting, crushes, and dating can have consequences for you, your reputation, and for any other tween who might be involved. So, it's important to think about your choices and their consequences.

TWEEN
POINTS

- Take your time to enjoy your crushes—you don't need to do anything other than enjoy the feelings!

- Once you tell other kids that you are attracted to someone, it may no longer be private.

- There will be time for dating in the future, even if you feel that this is not the right time now.

In this chapter, you read about having a crush, flirting, dating, fooling around, and the possible consequences of these choices. In addition, you were reminded that not rushing to date because of peer pressure, seeking guidance from trusted adults, figuring out who you are interested in, and having close friends or being in a group can be a great way to move through the tween years! In the next chapter, you will read about your tween social life. Enjoy!

CHAPTER SEVEN

FRIENDS, GROUPS, AND YOUR EVOLVING SOCIAL LIFE

You are unique! Maybe you really like to show others that you are a one-of-a-kind tween. At the same time, though, you may feel pressure to fit in and be like everyone else. Definitely a classic tween conundrum!

TAKE A MOMENT TO REVIEW THE ITEMS BELOW. COULD YOU SAY THESE THINGS ABOUT YOURSELF?

☐ I have a group of friends that fit me just right!

☐ I know how much I'm willing to change (or not) just to fit in.

☐ Even though sometimes I feel different, I still feel like I belong to a group.

☐ Sometimes I am a follower and other times I am a leader.

☐ I have made difficult decisions that I am proud of, even though my friends didn't always agree with me.

☐ Even when I feel different from others, I don't usually feel lonely.

☐ I am comfortable sometimes spending time by myself doing my own thing.

Wanting to be an individual and at the same time wanting not to stand out can be confusing and even stressful. Has this happened to you? Do you ever feel pulled in two different directions? Being yourself or being who others think you should be? Do you wonder about how to be your unique, wonderful self and yet not be so different that you draw unwanted attention to yourself?

During your tween years, it can be a challenge to figure out who you are, what you want, and to find a group of friends with whom you are comfortable hanging out, especially when you are changing and everyone is on a different tween timeline. You might not feel like your friends appreciate you for you and that they really want you to be exactly like them. The truth is that you can be *you* and still fit in with friends. But how? Read on to find out!

DO FRIENDSHIPS COME AND GO?

Now that you are a tween, you may suddenly find that you like to hang out with different friends. Maybe old friends have different interests now or have started spending time with other kids, too. Maybe you have met some new kids, in school or in new activities, with whom you really enjoy hanging out. Your long-time friendships may now seem different. Perhaps your BFF (best friend forever) has changed to a GFF (good friend forever), or even to a CAF (close acquaintance forever). While some of these letter abbreviations are made up, the concept may sound familiar. Friendships change. What doesn't when you are a tween, right?

It is okay to maintain a connection with a person who used to be a close friend, or even a best friend, but now is someone you consider to be an acquaintance. If you wish to do so, make time to hang out with your former BFF. You may have a long history together and may even consider yourselves like long-distance cousins—you don't see each other much, but when you do, you have a special bond. So it may make sense to hold onto this connection.

> the truth is that you can be *you* and still fit in with friends

If your former BFF seems to want more of your time and attention than you want to give, you may want to explain that you still value your time with him or her, but you also want time to get to know other kids and do new activities. This may be hard for your former best friend to understand and accept, though. Remember that you once were very close to this friend, so be thoughtful and caring as you work to change the relationship. For example, try to still make some time for this person, avoid telling jokes or personal stuff about him or her to others, and know that sometimes former BFFs later become BFFs again as tweens change. It's also helpful to think about how you would want to be treated if the roles were reversed, and your BFF now only wanted to be your acquaintance—try treating your former BFF how you would want to be treated.

> try new activities, get to know new kids, get to know more about what and who makes you feel happy

On the flip side, have you ever been in the position where you want to stay close friends with someone, but that person is moving on? Has your best friend dumped you? When this happens, tweens can feel rejected, hurt, sad, lonely, scared, angry, and a whole bunch of other emotions. Daphne wanted to hold onto her close connection with Chrissy. She kept hanging around Chrissy during lunch and in after-school clubs. Daphne tried to get Chrissy's attention when they were with a group of other kids by talking about things they used to do together. Guess what? Chrissy felt annoyed and wanted to end all contact with Daphne! "Everywhere I went, there was Daphne. Every time I tried to hang out with other kids, there was Daphne. I started to really dislike her. She seemed so desperate!"

So, if you feel left out or feel like you are losing a close friendship, what could you do? One thing is to pay attention to your former best friend's feelings and actions. Let your former friend know that you still want to hang out when you are both free—no need to sound like you are waiting around, though. If you feel that your former friend is hanging out with others because you accidentally hurt his or her feelings, try asking your friend about this privately. In addition, remember that you want to find friends who like hanging out with you, and you can't brainwash or force this person to want the friendship, no matter how hard you try! If you now have extra free time, because you are no longer with your friend, use this time in a fun way—try new activities, get to know new kids, get to know more about what and who makes you feel happy!

If you are still struggling with your feelings, try talking to trusted adults about the situation. They may have some helpful ideas for you.

MAKE NEW FRIENDS–ALWAYS AN OPTION

As a tween, there is a lot to consider when it comes to friendships. Take a minute to think about these questions:

- Can you have many great friends, not just one best friend?
- Can you still find time for former close friends, even though you aren't that close now?
- Do you know how to feel okay about who you are, even if your friendship is changing?
- How can you find more friends who are similar to you and share similar interests?
- If you are in a friendship, and can't be uniquely you and do things that feel safe and right to you, can you talk with your friend about this? Can you pull away if you feel disrespected or pressured to do things that you believe are unsafe or inappropriate?

TOTAL TWEEN MOMENT: JACOB'S STORY

Jacob and Ben were longtime friends. When they were younger they were inseparable. As they grew older, Jacob discovered that he loved playing lacrosse and flag football, but Ben was still into Pokémon and Xbox. When Jacob made the lacrosse team, he began to hang around with his teammates and didn't spend much time with Ben. At first, Jacob was fine with this because he wasn't into Pokémon and Xbox anymore. He felt that hanging out with Ben was boring because they had nothing in common. But eventually Jacob realized that Ben was still a good friend and he really liked Ben. Ben's sense of humor was just the same as his! Jacob began to spend some time with Ben playing football videogames like Madden NFL and even found a lacrosse video game that Ben liked too!

Has a situation like this ever happened to you or someone you know?

What do you think about how Jacob handled this experience?

What would you have done if you were Jacob?

How would you feel if you were Ben? What would you do?

If you are a tween who is interested in meeting new people and possibly making new friends, what can you do? Here are some ideas for how to meet new people:

- Figure out who you want to meet—is it someone who shares your interests or someone who simply seems nice and likes to have fun?

- Find a good time to introduce yourself. For example, when the other person is rushing off to class, it is probably not a good time to talk.

- Figure out a good way to introduce yourself. Casual is probably best. You could say something like, "Your art project is great. I love art and do watercolor paintings, too. How long have you been painting?" This way, you tell the other person about your interest and you give the other kid the chance to respond to a specific, but not too personal, question.

- Practice your introduction by talking into a mirror or by role-playing.

- Take it slow! Just because the other person may not respond exactly as you wanted, it doesn't mean that he or she hates you. It may mean that you need to go more slowly in getting to know each other.

- Three strikes and they are out! If you try to get to know someone casually three times, and there is no positive response, it's time to move on to someone else for now.

As you try to make new friends, remember that you want to find friends who work to get to know you as much as you work to get to know them!

KNOW-HOW NOW:

LEARN HOW TO BE FRIENDS

Did you know that learning about how to be friendly and get along with others starts at a very early age? Playing together is a way for young children to develop social skills. Even if someone hasn't developed super strong social skills, they can be taught. If you find yourself struggling to make friends, you can ask for help and you can learn! Ask your parents, older brothers or sisters, your teacher, the school psychologist, or other support people in your life for advice. Give it a try!

Lawhon, T. (1997). Encouraging friendships among children. *Childhood Education, 73,* 228–231.

BE A FOLLOWER, A LEADER...OR BOTH

In friendships, sometimes people take on roles where one person is always the leader and one person is always the follower. This may work in some friendships, but why limit yourself to being one or the other? Imagine that you are assigned to work on a social studies project with three other students in your class. Harold is super organized, Gloria loves to write, and Brittany loves drawing. Wouldn't you want to hear from each of these students about what ideas they have and what they could add to the project? You could also share your special talents or abilities and voice your recommendations in that area. In this case, there would not be a single leader, since everyone could lead in their area of expertise.

Listening to others and being open to their suggestions—but also sharing your ideas and plans for the project—can lead to a finished project that is special because it blends so many viewpoints, talents, and ideas. Since your friends are not exactly like you, they may have some experiences or knowledge that you do not have yet. For instance, your friends may play a sport or enjoy a game that you have never tried. They may even feel comfortable going to places that you have never been to before. If you feel like you want to join your friends, and you believe that the activity is not dangerous, try it! It's okay to ask friends or family members for guidance beforehand so that you understand what will happen, what the rules are, or how to handle the new experience.

Kids generally appreciate it when their friends are willing to join them for an activity, even though it's not the other friend's favorite thing in the world to do. Just knowing that you are important to your friends, they want to have your company, and you are willing to join them may make everyone feel good. Not joining your friends may lead to some hurt feelings and sometimes, even the loss of a close friendship.

> kids generally appreciate it when their friends are willing to join them for an activity

Sometimes however, it's wise *not* to join in activities (be a follower) and it's wise to leave a friendship. Imagine if your good friend wanted to start doing dangerous or inappropriate things—such as cutting class, using drugs, shoplifting, or acting like a bully. You might not feel comfortable doing these things and wouldn't want to have your reputation hurt. In this case, it would be a good idea to distance yourself from that friend. You could tell your friend that you might want the friendship back, if he or she starts to make choices that make you more comfortable.

Remember that you are an important person and you want to find friends who respect and appreciate you. Do you also respect and appreciate your friends? You will know you have found a good connection if you and the other person enjoy each other's company, have some similar interests, and don't try to brainwash each other into thinking in one particular way.

HANG WITH GROUPS OF FRIENDS

Do you already have a group of friends who all hang out together? Think about the kids you know—do kids with similar interests tend to group together? Or do kids group together for other reasons? Or both? Sometimes it's confusing to know what you want, how you feel, what goals you have, and which group of friends is the best fit for you. Take a minute to think about your group of friends, and try answering the following questions:

- Do you feel that you can relax and be yourself around the group?
- Do you have common interests with the other kids in the group?
- Do you like the reputation that the group has and the way they treat others?
- Can you keep other friends, yet still be accepted in this group?

Being part of a group can be fun! The group can be just boys, just girls, or a mix of both. Some kids in groups date. Some groups don't focus on dating at all. Make sure that the group you are in feels like a good fit for you. Do you enjoy the group? Are you accepted for being you in the group? Do you still have time for hanging out with kids outside of the group? If the answer is "yes," then you have found a group that works for you!

being part of a group can be fun

If not, is it time to move away from that group? How much are you willing to change or what will you do just to fit in? These are not easy questions to answer. Even adults don't always know the answer when it comes to fitting in with their friends or social group.

A lot of times, group members try to think and act the same way, so everyone in the group feels comfortable that they are just like each other and that they are "okay" and "normal." You may even notice that kids in some groups start to act, talk, and dress alike. When a group of friends hang out a lot together and feel that they are close and have a special bond together, they are sometimes referred to as a "clique." Unfortunately, that isn't necessarily a good thing. The term "clique" is often used to describe a group with some not-so-good qualities, such as excluding others.

Have you ever sat on a seesaw with another person around your weight sitting opposite you and then tried to balance the seesaw so it stays perfectly horizontal? It's not an easy thing to do. It's like that with groups. Finding a perfect balance between presenting yourself to the world as a one-of-a-kind person and presenting yourself as a person who is similar to other kids in your group can be tricky.

You may experience some peer pressure to stick with your group of friends, be loyal to them, and be just like them. Think about how you fit into your group:

- Do you hide your unique qualities because you want to fit in?
- If you recorded yourself while you were hanging out with your friends, would you feel like you were acting naturally or just acting?
- Do you frequently try to teach your friends about your particular interests or thoughts and try to convince them to be just like you?
- Do you work extra hard to be different from other people just to let them know that you are unique?
- Do you feel you can be true to your own personality and values and also join others in sharing activities and jokes?
- Overall, do you feel that your seesaw has a nice balance?

If you answered "yes" to the last two items, congratulations! You can appreciate that no one is exactly like you and also enjoy being one of a group.

If you are still working on finding balance, you are not alone. Just be aware when you work too hard to fit in and ask yourself "Why?"

What happens if your friends start to act differently or do things you don't like to do? It might be time to move on, or break up with your group and find new friends. Choosing friends because they fit well with your own personality and goals is a sign of maturity.

Penelope enjoyed classical music. She often downloaded music from iTunes or listened to classical music on Internet radio stations. When her friends found out, they began teasing her. One friend even said, "Is your grandfather brainwashing you with that stuff? We'll have to cure you of this problem." Penelope just smiled and said, "I like it. Try it. Maybe it will grow on you." Penelope and her friends had a lot of other interests in common, and Penelope made it clear that she wasn't going to give up her music, so they simply agreed to disagree about their musical tastes.

What do you think of Penelope's response to her friends' teasing?

Have you ever had different interests than your group of friends?

Has something similar happened to you?

If so, how did you handle it?

If you find yourself in a situation where you don't feel like you fit with your group of friends, here are some things to keep in mind when looking for your new group of friends:

- Find a group of kids with whom you share common interests.
- Make sure the kids you want as friends also like and appreciate you.
- Think about whether you are proud to admit you hang out with these kids. For example, would you be comfortable letting your old friends and your parents know who you want to spend time with?
- Be yourself. If you have to "act" rather than be yourself in order to be accepted by the new kids, this probably isn't the best group for you.

As you try to make new friends, be true to what you think is right. If you feel like you have to try behaviors that you feel are wrong—such as smoking pot, drinking, and cheating on tests—just to fit in, try a different group.

When Joseph was younger, he hung out with the kids on his block and kids whose parents were friends with his. Now, at the age of twelve, he wanted to hang out with the guys who joked around a lot in the cafeteria and "seemed cool."

Joseph decided that his old friends were nerds and he was ready to join the new group. To prove to the "cool" kids that he was ready to fit in, he laughed a lot at their jokes and shared his homework answers when they asked. Later, he even acted like he was happy when he learned that one of the guys took a picture of the answer key to their upcoming math test.

Joseph believed that he was smart, honest, and responsible. He had never cheated before. However, he ended up letting his new friend send him the answer key photo because he wanted to be accepted by this group. He never actually used it, but he felt guilty and uncomfortable even having the photo. He started to feel like he was no longer smart, since he took the answer key, and he wasn't being honest and responsible. He was having trouble sleeping and didn't know what to do—he wanted to do anything necessary to keep his new friends, and he wanted to do what he thought was right. Unfortunately, he wasn't sure that he could do both.

Eventually, Joseph confided in his father about his dilemma. At first, his father was upset by Joseph's behavior, but he quickly calmed down. To Joseph's surprise, once calm, his father said, "Thank you for telling me about this. It actually shows I can trust you. Now let's figure out how to deal with this problem." After talking with his dad, Joseph realized that he was so focused on this new group that he had ignored his large group of friends who always appreciated him without pressuring him to do things that made him uncomfortable. He then spent the next week apologizing to his old friends and asking them to give him another chance. He decided to continue to talk with and even laugh with some of the new kids sometimes, but he avoided doing the things that didn't feel right to him just to fit in. Joseph had now found a way to balance his seesaw!

How do you think Joseph handled the situation?

Has anything like this happened to you? If so, what did you do?

ALONE OR LONELY?

Being alone and being lonely are not the same thing! If you are alone in your bedroom, you may feel lonely, wishing that you were out with other people. However, you may also feel happy that you are alone and can just spend time by yourself. While some kids may think that it isn't "normal" to want to be alone, lots of tweens love having the chance to spend time in their room or just do their own things! In fact, spending time alone can be very important. It allows you to get to know your changing self, relax, and focus on your hobbies, interests, and goals.

Many tweens are busy with Facebook, Instagram, texting, FaceTime, or Skype, and they forget that even though they may be alone in their room, they are not truly by themselves. So unplug from technology for a while and hang out with you! Try doing homework by yourself, reading, listening to music, drawing, journaling, or doing other activities that relax you, that you enjoy, and that don't involve another person. Sometimes, this can be uncomfortable at the beginning, if you aren't used to it, but it gets easier over time.

On the other hand, some kids can be surrounded by friends, yet still feel lonely. If this happens to you, think about whether you are feeling lonely because you are feeling different from your friends at that time. Are they laughing when you want to be serious? Are they serious when you want to just joke around?

> lots of tweens love having the chance to spend time in their room or just do their own things

Sometimes feeling different or unique can lead to confidence and pride. Other times, it can lead to feeling lonely. If you find a nice balance between being comfortable with being different and being comfortable with friends, then occasional differences may not lead to you feeling lonely. If you are constantly lonely when you are in a group, do you know why? Do you have anything in common with the others? If not, are there kids you might connect with more and won't feel lonely around?

Some tweens find that they feel lonely no matter where they are, who they are with, or what they are doing. If this describes you, are you usually also feeling down or depressed? If you rarely enjoy activities, people around you, or even yourself, then speak up. Talk to an adult about your feelings. While the tween years may be confusing, you don't want to constantly feel sad or nervous during this journey. It may be time to speak to a professional, who has worked with tons of tweens, and can offer you some expert suggestions.

TOTAL TWEEN MOMENT: BELLA'S STORY

Bella felt good hanging out with her friends. However, one day, she felt lonely because her friends were all excited and were talking about a movie. Bella felt that the movie was boring, and shared this with the other kids. They tried to explain why they still loved the movie, then turned back to each other and kept talking about how amazing the movie was. Bella slowly walked away from her friends and, later, told her mother, "They didn't pay any attention to me just because I had a different idea about the movie. I felt invisible." Bella's mother said, "Dad and I sometimes have different opinions, but because we listen to each other, we don't feel alone. Your friends did seem to listen to your comment. But you walked away."

Can you understand why Bella felt lonely?

Has this happened to you?

If so, what did you do?

What could Bella have done to stay connected to the discussion and her friends?

TWEEN POINTS

- Friendships come, go, sometimes last forever, but sometimes change.

- Find a group with whom you share common interests and in which the kids you want as friends will like and appreciate you.

- If you want to spend some time alone, you're not weird, and you won't necessarily feel lonely!

In this chapter, you read about how to handle changing friendships and ways to fit in with a group of friends, even while you are comfortable being unique and not identical to anyone else. But what if there are problems in your social life? In the next chapter, you will have a chance to read about how to handle social situations that lead to hurt feelings, teasing, bullying, and other not-so-fun (and even painful) experiences.

CHAPTER EIGHT

MAJOR CONFLICTS AND PROBLEMS IN YOUR SOCIAL LIFE

Some tweens enjoy every minute of their social lives. However, difficult social situations happen to a lot of kids. In your own social life, have you ever encountered rumors, gossip, lies, teasing, or even bullying?

TAKE A MINUTE TO READ THROUGH THE ITEMS BELOW. DO ANY OF THEM REFLECT THINGS YOU'VE DONE OR THOUGHT?

☐ If my feelings are hurt by friends, I am able to talk it out with them.

☐ I have some strategies for dealing with an acquaintance teasing me.

☐ I don't jump to conclusions based on what someone tells me another kid said.

☐ I can confide in my parents and ask for their help and support.

☐ I know how to handle bullying.

☐ I have some strategies for dealing with peer pressure.

☐ I know how to keep myself safe online.

In this chapter, you'll learn some coping strategies for dealing with social conflicts and mistreatment. Also, if you find that you have mistreated others, for example, by teasing or gossiping, you will have an opportunity to think about this and work to change your behavior so others don't feel hurt by your actions.

LIES, RUMORS, AND TEASING

Have you ever told a fib? Have you ever teased a friend and not meant to hurt her feelings? Have you ever shared gossip or rumors that you felt were harmless? Have you ever intentionally lied in an effort to *not* hurt someone's feelings? The truth is that it isn't always easy to know if fibbing, teasing, or gossiping will be hurtful to another person.

Sometimes, in a situation, the teasing or fibbing turns out to be funny or harmless. Other times, a person may feel deceived, lied to, or upset about being teased. In fact, a friendship could end if someone is upset enough about the lies, rumors, or teasing. So what should you do?

> friends are supposed to be there to make you feel good, support you, and encourage you

Friends are supposed to be there to make you feel good, support you, and encourage you. Right? Well, that's what friends generally try to do. But just like with brothers and sisters, sometimes it doesn't always work out that way. When friends (or siblings) are together a lot, sometimes disagreements or even jealousy can develop. Sometimes friends tease each other or otherwise hurt each other's feelings.

Friends may not always be aware that they are hurting another friend's feelings. This probably happens more often than a friend hurting you intentionally. For example, if you believe that friends should Skype each other every night, and your friend doesn't think this is important, your friend might accidentally hurt your feelings by not contacting you.

Friends may hurt each other for a whole bunch of reasons. Colin lied to his friend Alex by saying that he wasn't invited to a party because he didn't want Alex to realize that he was the only one who didn't get an invitation. In this situation, Colin felt that he was actually protecting Alex by lying.

> friends may not always be aware that they are hurting another friend's feelings

Here are a few other reasons why tweens have lied, teased, or spread rumors:

- To fit in with a group.
- To have a certain reputation. For example, Maya lied and said, "I dated a boy at summer camp," so her friends would think she was cool.
- To be looked up to by friends. For example, Jack told his friends, "I built this robot all by myself," instead of admitting his dad and older sister helped.
- To prove they are popular by sharing information about other kids to show how much they know about so many people.

If you have a friend who hurts you frequently by teasing, spreading rumors or telling lies, you may want to think about whether this person is a good friend or just someone you like to hang around sometimes. If this person is a good friend, it might help to talk to him or her. But if this person is someone you just like to hang with occasionally and don't truly trust, maybe it is time to take a break from the friendship. Even though it's not easy to admit when a person you like isn't treating you well, it's important that you don't stay in a relationship where you are mistreated.

Keep in mind that you are not to blame if rumors or lies are started about you. Perhaps your friend is jealous that a girl he has a crush on likes you more than him, so he takes it out on you. Or maybe your friend is envious of your grades in math class and decides to spread untrue stories about you without thinking of the cost to your friendship. Tweens can feel very lonely, scared, embarrassed, or confused when a friend spreads lies, starts rumors, tells secrets, or teases them. If this ever happens to you, you may want to retreat back to your younger years when life seemed simpler. Rather than running away from your tweens, though, it's helpful to try to figure out what is going on and what to do about it.

> keep in mind that you are not to blame if rumors or lies are started about you

Have you ever had a friend tell you what another kid said about you? This is what's known as "the messenger game." Even if your friend accurately related the information to you, your friend may have misunderstood the meaning behind the words or the reason for the words. Cory, for instance, heard from Dwain that Liam thought he was always hogging the ball in soccer. Cory was hurt and angry. He told Dwain, "Maybe I wouldn't 'hog the ball' so much if Liam was better at soccer. Tell him that I think he should get off the team if he can't handle me being so talented!"

Guess what? Dwain went to Liam and said, "Cory wanted you to know that he thinks you stink at soccer, so he has to play extra hard to cover for you." What do you think happened next? Cory and Liam were furious with each other for almost a week before they finally talked it out. Dwain thought he was helping, but he ended up just complicating the situation.

If you ever hear things through a messenger, remember that it's like the game of telephone—what was heard and repeated may not be exactly what was originally said or meant!

If a friend starts telling lies, rumors, or secrets about you, you may not know what to do and you may not know whom to talk to about it. Luckily, there are strategies that have worked for other kids and might work for you, too:

- Try to figure out when the hurtful things started to happen and why things changed in this way. This may help you to understand what's going on.

- If a friend is saying hurtful things, try to think about whether your friend might be upset with you. When you are alone with this friend—so there is no audience!—ask if you have accidentally hurt him or her.

- If you talk it out, try using "I" messages like "I feel…" to say what you feel rather than "you" messages or accusatory statements like "Why are *you* acting so weird?"

- Keep in mind that while you may think some kids are whispering about you, they may be whispering about something that has nothing to do with you. If that's the case, politely ask them to talk about it when you aren't around.

- Keep an open mind. Jumping to conclusions may lead to even more miscommunication. If you generally trust your friends, try trusting what they tell you, unless you have reason to believe they are no longer trustworthy.

- Remember that no one deserves to be teased, ridiculed, or mistreated—that includes you!

These strategies can help if a friend is teasing you or spreading rumors about you. But what can you do if kids you don't even know well are teasing you or spreading rumors or lies about you?

They might be doing it on purpose to hurt your feelings, or just joking around. But either way, it can still hurt a lot. You may still feel like crying or screaming. It can seem so unfair! Here are some tips if you feel that you are being teased by an acquaintance:

- If you feel that the kid is generally a nice person, don't tease back, but say, "You seem like a nice kid. Why are you teasing me?"
- Stand up for yourself without teasing the other person back and say, "Chill! That's so not cool!" or "Wow, you sure notice me a lot!"
- Hang with friends who make you feel good—kids in groups are harder to tease than kids who are alone.
- If the teasing isn't super serious, smile and walk away.

If you find yourself having to deal with rumors, lies, or gossip, your hurt feelings and stress may feel overwhelming. At these times, it can be helpful to share your feelings with an adult you trust.

Some tweens are afraid to talk with their parents because they don't want their parents to call the parents of the other child or the principal. If that is how you feel, let your parents know that you are looking for suggestions on what *you* can do and are not looking for them to handle the situation for you. Other adults can also help, such as your school guidance counselor, a teacher, or the school psychologist.

It's always helpful to remember how much these actions can hurt. You have the power to spare others these hurt feelings by not starting or spreading rumors, lies, or teasing. If you find that you are teasing someone else:

- Realize that knowing that you are teasing is the first step toward stopping.
- Ask yourself, "How would I feel if someone did this to me?" But remember that another person might be hurt, even if you wouldn't be.
- Ask yourself, "Do I really want to hurt this person?" If the answer is "yes," ask yourself "why." If "no," ask yourself why you are doing it.
- Practice things you can say to this person that won't be hurtful, but won't make you uncomfortable either.

Remember that words that leave your mouth can't be taken back. Since your reputation is often based on what you do and say, take a moment to think about whether you are teasing or hurting someone and how it might influence how others view you.

BULLIES AND BYSTANDERS BEWARE!

Bullying is a serious problem. No kid ever wants or deserves to be bullied! How is bullying different from just teasing? One characteristic of bullying is an imbalance of power. The kid that is being bullied generally feels or actually is less powerful—either physically or socially—than the person doing the bullying. Also, the behavior is repeated over time, or it is so hurtful that it is considered serious.

There are many different kinds of bullying. Some examples of bullying include physical aggression, repeated negative and insulting comments, ridicule, or exclusion. Bullying can happen face-to-face or even online. If you still are not sure what bullying is, think about other people's behavior as if it's on a continuum. At one end are the supportive actions of friends. Not far from that is gentle teasing between friends that doesn't actually hurt either friend's feelings. Next are teasing, gossiping, or rumor spreading that hurt someone. At the far end of the continuum are things that make you really, really uncomfortable or scared. Bullying is at the serious end of that continuum.

So, why do kids bully other kids? Some kids pick on other kids, but stop once they are spoken to because they just never thought about the feelings of the kid they are picking on. Some kids act like bullies to be accepted by a particular group of friends. Other kids might bully to show that they are popular, powerful, and confident and have lots of friends to support them (these friends might laugh when they witness the bullying). Still other kids might have anger because of a situation in their personal life, may have friends that bully others, have difficulty following rules, think badly of others, or have other reasons.

It may feel like it is hard to talk about, but if you are being bullied, it is important to tell an adult about what is happening so the adult can keep an eye out. Some schools may first just increase supervision when you and the person bullying you are together, such as in class or at lunch. Some schools may speak to the other student and his or her parents.

Aaron was being bullied by Ryan. Ryan would punch or push Aaron whenever he walked past him in the hallway, and would call him insulting names so that the other kids would start to laugh. At first, Aaron tried telling his parents that he was sick so that he could miss school. He tried to tell Ryan to cut it out. He tried to ask his friends for help, but they admitted that they didn't want to interfere because they didn't want Ryan to bully them.

Aaron ended up talking with his parents about Ryan. At first, his parents wanted to call Ryan's parents and ask them to talk with their son. However, Aaron asked them not to do this. They met with the principal the next morning to see what the school staff suggested. The principal had not known about the bullying and was glad to learn about it so that he could help Aaron. He ended up reviewing the videos from the school cameras, and saw some times when Ryan punched and pushed Aaron. He brought Ryan and his parents into his office to meet with him. Aaron was never blamed for telling anyone about the situation. If this hadn't worked, Aaron knew that the principal had other ideas. Aaron also knew that his friends were now willing to speak up, as a group, to tell Ryan to "Stop!" In addition, Aaron learned that if he were ever seriously threatened, his parents would get guidance from the neighborhood police.

How do you think Aaron handled the situation?

Has something similar happened to you or someone you know?

Here are some other things to do if you are bullied:

- Remind yourself that no one deserves to be bullied. It's not your fault, ever.
- Look at the bully and tell him or her to stop (if you believe that it is safe to do this).
- If speaking up to the bully is too hard or feels unsafe, walk away and find an adult.
- Don't fight back.

- Hang with a group of friends or stick near adults. Bullying most often happens when someone is alone.

- Let the person bullying you know that you do not think his or her actions are funny or cool. Only do this if the kid isn't being physically aggressive or dangerous.

- Talk to a trusted adult. Bullying is not something to keep private. Let adults know what is happening so they can help out. Even though you may not want to worry your parents, bullying is serious and your parents should be told.

Often bullying can stop if the bystanders—the kids who aren't being directly bullied but know about the bullying behavior or witness bullying incidents—take a stand. Some bystanders may unintentionally encourage the bullying behavior by laughing or by watching and doing nothing when the bullying happens. By laughing or doing nothing, bystanders allow the bullying to continue and may lead the bully to believe that he or she is supported and that the bullying is okay because no one is doing anything to stop the actions.

So here is your challenge. Can you be an upstanding bystander? What can you do if you witness bullying? Here are some tips:

- Don't give the kid who bullies an audience, encourage his or her behavior, or laugh when he or she bullies another kid.

- Try saying "Stop!" or "Chill!" or "Hey, we like her."

- Help the kid who is being bullied get away. You can simply say, "Hey, aren't you supposed to be in the art club now?" or "I was looking all over for you. Come on, we're late for class and have to hand in our project."

- If you are friends with the kid doing the bullying, you may be able to have an honest conversation about how the behaviors make you uncomfortable and you want them to stop.

- Be a friend to the kid who is bullied. Include this person with your group or with you. You could invite him or her to do something with you after school or sit with you at lunch. Hanging out together will let the person know you care and do not agree with the kid who is bullying him or her. Also, he or she will be less likely to be picked on while in a group.

- Speak up. Individually or as part of a group, you can report what has been going on to school staff or to your parents. Bullying can be very serious and sometimes requires adults to step in to deal with it.

Someone who bullies another person may eventually change and no longer hurt others (after receiving consequences or support). There are even some kids who just have a realization in the tween years that they no longer want to treat others badly, or decide that they want to develop a more positive reputation.

However, don't wait for time to pass and hope that the bullying will eventually stop. Ask for help now to make the situation end and to assure that you and others are safe—today!

IS PEER PRESSURE ALWAYS NEGATIVE?

Have you ever felt pressure from friends to act in a certain way, take a dare, or share their opinions? Peer pressure can create stress for some tweens who are uncomfortable with what their friends are doing or what their friends want them to do.

Did you know that peer pressure can actually be helpful, at times? Sometimes friends may put pressure on another friend to take a risk, such as trying out for the school musical or going out for the track team. Other times friends could push you to do your best in school activities and help you to see the benefits of trying things you might not feel comfortable doing. Sometimes it's a good idea to give in to this kind of peer pressure.

> peer pressure can actually be helpful, at times

Other kinds of peer pressure are not as helpful, and might get you in trouble. This is usually what people talk about when they refer to peer pressure. It's when other kids put pressure on you to do something that doesn't feel safe to you or may go against your goals or values. An example of this kind of peer pressure might be to cheat on a test, spread a rumor, or even to try drugs.

Did you know that the more a tween wants the approval of the other kids, the more difficult it might be to handle these situations?

USING FAMILY RULES

Lots of parents have rules about tween behaviors. For example, some kids can't watch PG-13 movies without their parents' approval, or must check in with their parent if they go someplace that's not part of the typical after-school routine. While parents are trying to keep their children safe, sometimes family rules can create tension.

Many tweens seek freedom and want to make their own decisions, while parents often want to set some boundaries or restrictions on how much independence is allowed.

Parents often know about peer pressure and know that tweens might be facing situations that they aren't ready for or that go against family rules. Having firm family rules can help a tween deal with peer pressure from friends or other groups of kids.

TOTAL TWEEN MOMENT: NADIA'S STORY

When Nadia turned twelve, her friends started having parties where kids were kissing, trying beer, and daring each other to take unhealthy risks.

Nadia talked to her father about this. She said, "I want to tell you something. My friends are all trying to act like stupid teenagers. I don't want to but I don't want to lose all my friends, either. I don't want anyone to think I'm some kind of loser. What should I do?"

Nadia's father told her, "Try this trick. It worked for me when I was your age. Blame your mom and me. Tell your friends that we are annoying parents. Tell them that the only parties that we'll allow are ones in our house with us present."

What do you think of Nadia using family rules to avoid peer pressure?

Would this work for you?

SOCIAL LIFE WITH SOCIAL MEDIA

Social media can be a great way to stay connected with others. Tweens connect with their friends on Instagram, Twitter, or Pinterest. Maybe you have a YouTube channel or do Vine videos. Kids use the Internet for researching group projects, doing homework, emailing their teachers questions or homework, or just surfing around for fun.

But with such great technology, there are also risks! Do you wonder why so many adults caution you about social media and Internet use?

Parents worry that there could be an adult pretending to be a child, even a friend of yours, in order to earn your trust and potentially mistreat you.

Parents also worry about your reputation, your "brand," and how you display yourself publicly (and remember, anything online is never truly private).

If you post something about yourself or others, once it is "out there," you have no control over it—your words, videos, or pictures could be shared or sent around to anyone, maybe even to some people who you wish didn't get it.

Additionally, you could unintentionally hurt someone's feelings whom you never meant to hurt.

> **if you post something about yourself or others, once it is "out there," you have no control over it**

You may text friends a sarcastic or silly comment and because they don't hear the tone of your voice, they may misunderstand you.

Avoid sending photos or videos that can embarrass you, get you in trouble, hurt someone's feelings, or that are inappropriate or rude.

Don't post pictures of your friends without their permission, and ask that they also check with you first before posting photos or videos of you. You never really know who will see them or if the images will be passed along to another person.

A good rule of thumb is that if you wouldn't want your parents, teachers, grandparents, or principal to see your photos or videos, don't post them!

Similarly, avoid texting comments you wouldn't say in front of adults—remember that your typed words can be forwarded to others without you knowing.

Someday you may be applying for college. You wouldn't want an admissions director to see an embarrassing or inappropriate photo or read your rude or silly comments, right?

> If you wouldn't want your parents, teachers, grandparents, or principal to see your photos or videos, don't post them

Finally, bullying someone online is called cyberbullying. Just like face-to-face bullying, it is aggressive and hurtful! Some kids find that it's easy to insult or hurt others online or by text message when they don't have to look at their hurt reaction or look at them face-to-face.

In addition to not sending around very personal texts, posting embarrassing pictures or comments, or spreading misinformation, it's important not to share passwords, your real name, address, phone number, the name of your school, or other identifying information with other tweens or adults online. You never really know who is getting the information.

Also, never text or post messages that your parents aren't home or that you are on vacation. Since you don't know who might read your post, you don't want to publicly share such information. It's a matter of safety!

> Bullying someone online is called cyberbullying. Just like face-to-face bullying, it is aggressive and hurtful

TWEEN
POINTS

- Bullying (including cyberbullying) is never okay!

- Become an upstanding bystander—you can make a difference!

- If a friend hurts your feelings, take your time, then talk it out.

In this chapter, you learned about some ways to handle lies, teasing, and rumors by friends or just kids you know. Remember that you have the power to protect other kids by not teasing or spreading rumors and lies about them. The very serious issue of bullying and ways of dealing with it were also discussed. Safety tips for using social media were reviewed as well. In the next chapter, you will read about tips to help you to deal with school now that some of the expectations might be changing as you move into higher grades.

CHAPTER NINE

SCHOOLWORK, CHANGING EXPECTATIONS, AND LIFELONG LEARNING

Now that you have learned basic math, spelling, writing, and reading skills, your teachers' expectations of you may change. While these skills are still important, your teachers may now expect you to write essays about topics discussed in class and may assume that you already know how to spell and write paragraphs accurately.

TAKE A MINUTE TO READ THROUGH THESE ITEMS. DO ANY OF THESE STATEMENTS DESCRIBE WHAT YOU ALREADY DO?

☐ I know how to put ideas into my own words, and attribute quotes and ideas that I got from somewhere else.

☐ I already have some effective organizational skills for keeping track of assignments.

☐ I know the environment in which I study best.

☐ I know how to prioritize my work so I finish assignments before the due date.

☐ I make sure my schedule includes time for studying and time for relaxing.

Schoolwork and even homework expectations may change. Not only that, teachers (and parents) often will encourage you to be more independent as you complete your work. You may be expected to take notes in class, research topics for projects, or choose books for independent reading. Studying and homework probably become your responsibility, too.

This chapter will show you some strategies to cope with your teachers' changing expectations of you. You will learn about ways to stay organized and how to find the best spot for you to study and do your homework. In addition, you will read about study skills that will help you throughout your life, even after you leave school!

DEALING WITH MORE SCHOOL ASSIGNMENTS AND RESPONSIBILITIES

Remember the old days? Your third grade teacher may have asked you to complete a sheet of math problems, write out spelling words three times, and then write each of them in a sentence in your notebook. Pretty straightforward, right? Well, now you may have to do science research projects, create PowerPoint presentations, record conversation skits for your Spanish class, or maybe even write an essay about what it was like to live in ancient Greece (or whatever period of history that you are studying). These assignments can be more interesting and a lot of fun, but they take much more thought and time.

You now probably have more teachers and more work. Teachers may give assignments or tests on the same day as other teachers. You might have long-term projects, quizzes, and tests to think about now. Your social life may be buzzing with activity, too. Maybe you are busy with music lessons, sports practices, or after-school hobbies. Your life may be busier than ever! At times, this can be overwhelming, frustrating, annoying, or even make you worry. You may wish to return to the old days of kindergarten, when you didn't have to deal with so many responsibilities. However, there are things you can do to help you to deal with the increased work, and hopefully feel a lot less stress: prioritize your homework and activities, keep to a schedule, and organize all of your assignments.

TOTAL TWEEN MOMENT: JULIA'S STORY

Julia learned all about Egyptian civilization in her sixth grade class. Her assignment was to create a PowerPoint presentation for her class about the tombs of Egyptian kings. In order to add something original to her presentation, she also made a papier-mâché example of the tombs so everyone could see how the kings were buried.

Julia used her writing, spelling, and reading skills to prepare for this project. She had to pay attention to her writing to make sure her presentation was organized and her spelling was accurate. She also needed to research the tombs by reading a lot of books and looking at a number of websites. She broke down the project into manageable steps, and created a schedule so she could get everything done that she needed to do. Her schoolwork felt very different to her now that she needed to learn about things independently, in greater detail.

Julia admitted, "I used to be a little bored in school before I got to do research and presentations. Now, I get to go online sometimes and get even more information about topics that I like. I like school so much more now, although sometimes I really hate how much time my homework takes when I get so interested that I end up researching more than I need to."

Do you think creating a schedule for the project was a good idea?

Have you felt the same way as Julia?

Would this plan work for you?

PRIORITIZING BY DUE DATE

To keep on top of your day-to-day homework and assignments, you will need to learn to prioritize your work. One way to do this is by due date. When you have a lot of schoolwork, figure out what needs to be done now, what needs to be done soon, and what can wait until later. For example, if your math homework is due tomorrow and your social studies assignment is due three days from now, the math homework is top priority and you should do that homework first. After you complete your math homework, you may also want to do a little of your social studies assignment if it is lengthy. This way, you don't feel the pressure of completing a long assignment entirely the night before it is due to be handed in at school.

This might sound like obvious advice—do the homework that is due soon first. Sometimes, though, kids prioritize their work differently. Do you tend to do easier assignments or focus on studying or assignments that you like instead of doing what is due first? If so, you are not alone. However, if you spend your time prioritizing by what you like to do, you might end up running out of time to do a less enjoyable assignment that is due the next day. One way to make sure that you make all your deadlines is to complete things in order of when they are due.

PRIORITIZING BY IMPORTANCE

Sometimes you may have two or three school assignments that are due on the same day, or you might have other activities that are competing for your time. If this is the case, figure out what is most important for you to do right now.

For instance, imagine your friends are going to get together this weekend for a long sleepover. But you have a big final exam in science on Monday morning. This test can't be made up because it is the final test and it only happens once. Sleepovers can usually happen anytime, or as often as you plan them (and parents allow!). You may want to go to the sleepover, but if you do, will you have time to study for the science final? If you get a low grade on the science final would you regret going to the sleepover? Is there a way to do both?

to keep on top of your day-to-day homework and assignments, you will need to learn to prioritize your work

This is tricky because sometimes what is more important is not always what you want to do most. It might be helpful to talk to you parents or teachers about prioritizing your activities if you are having trouble deciding what needs to be done first.

Here are some things to keep in mind to help you deal with homework and tests:

- Prioritize your work to make sure that you finish assignments and studying before the due date.

- Figure out what is most important for you to focus on right now. Is it going to a party, or studying? Is it working on a science project due next month, or finishing an essay due tomorrow?

- If you have two tests on the same day, schedule time to study for each test over several days so that you have time to study for both and your brain doesn't get overloaded with too much information to memorize at once.

- Talk with friends to see how they manage to finish all of their schoolwork.

- If you are really overwhelmed, ask your teachers if there is any way to take the test or finish an assignment on a different day. Ask well in advance of the due date and be clear as to why this is an unusual situation and you won't plan on asking for additional extensions later.

If you aren't sure if you are prepared for a test, or not sure if you can finish your homework, don't avoid it. Sometimes you may think that a good strategy is simply to find an excuse to stay home from school when a test is coming up or an assignment is due. Remind yourself that it might feel good to stay home that day, but the next day things won't be better. You'll be behind in your work, and you'll still have to take the test or hand in the project.

GETTING ORGANIZED

Tween life can get pretty busy. You may be able to easily remember all your daily and weekly activities—like soccer practice, music lessons, and family plans—and what night you do those things. You might also remember what homework you need to do each night. But do yourself a favor. Use a notebook or planner to record all of your homework assignments and after-school activities. While you may have a great memory for information, it can be hard to keep track of your day-to-day homework and short-term assignments. Writing it all down, along with after-school activities and family plans or responsibilities, is extra protection against accidentally forgetting something.

Before leaving class, take a minute or two to make sure that you write down the assignments or the dates of upcoming tests. Writing down all of your homework and test dates can help you to stay organized. You only have to look in one place to find out what you need to do at home. You will need this planner to record homework and project due dates as well as when tests will occur for each class, so keep it in a separate section of your backpack where you can just grab it before the end of each class period.

What if you forget the planner at home one day? If this happens, write down all the homework and test dates given out that day on a single piece of paper and store it where you normally keep your planner. When you get home, copy the information into your planner!

You will also probably need a way to remember long-term projects and other responsibilities that don't occur weekly. A planner can help with this, too! What if you have a big research project that isn't due for four weeks? Maybe you have broken down this big project into ten smaller tasks and decided when you want to finish each smaller section. You could then add these steps into your planner so you remember to do them along with your daily homework. Also, on each Monday (or any day you prefer, but once a week), write a reminder of when the project is due, so you keep remembering the target date to finish the assignment.

Keeping a calendar may not be the most exciting thing you ever do, but it may take some pressure off of you when you realize that you are getting short-term and long-term assignments all done by their due dates! You can use a calendar that has one page for each day, one page for each week, or even a large month-at-a-glance calendar on a single paper.

MAKING YOUR OWN SCHEDULE

Even though it seems like a lot of work at first, you might try writing out a schedule of what you plan to do at certain times before and after school. You may be surprised at how much time you spend working without relaxing (or vice versa!). It often helps to see everything you want to do all laid out in one place. This can help you plan your work, pace yourself, and get it all done! Once you plan out your schedule, you can see if there is a need to make any changes.

Take a look at Becca's schedule for the week of March 2nd. She first listed the times she has soccer, astronomy club, family time, and music lessons. Then she plugged into her schedule things that she needed to or wanted to do for the upcoming week, such as: memorize new vocabulary words, work on sections 4 and 5 of her science project (due in a month), watch her younger sister's basketball game, study for her social studies test on Friday, and make time to relax or socialize (either online or in person with friends)!

BECCA'S SCHEDULE: MARCH 2-8

	SUNDAY	MONDAY	TUESDAY	WEDNESDAY	THURSDAY	FRIDAY	SATURDAY
7:30am-4:00pm	9-9:30—work on science project 9:30-10:30 work on speech for student council	school & travel time	school & travel time	school & travel time	school & travel time	school & travel time	9-11 soccer
4:00-5:00pm	relax	soccer practice	astronomy club	soccer practice	soccer practice	see friends	relax
5:00-5:30pm	chores	relax	relax	relax	relax	see friends	relax
5:30-6:30pm	relax	work on science project & do math sheet	math sheet & study for social studies test	math sheet & study for social studies test	math sheet & study for social studies test	see friends	relax
6:30-7:00pm	relax & dinner	dinner & family time	dinner & family time	dinner & family time	dinner & family time	dinner & family time	relax & dinner
7:00-8:00pm	relax	music lesson	relax	relax	watch Angie's basketball game	relax	see friends or just relax
8:00-9:00pm	relax	memorize ½ vocab words	memorize ½ vocab words	review vocab words	relax	relax	see friends or just relax
9:00-9:30pm	relax	relax	practice speech with parents	revise speech, as needed	relax	relax	practice speech for student council
10:00-10:30pm	read, then sleep	read, then sleep	read, then sleep	read, then sleep	read, then sleep	relax	relax

Becca's schedule looks pretty busy, right? When Becca first started making schedules, she forgot to include down time and time to relax. She also forgot to think about how long each part of her homework would take. As you can see from her current schedule, Becca now makes sure to include time devoted to relaxing and she tries to be specific about how long assignments will take to complete.

Take some time to create your own schedule for the next week. It may help to first list all that you need to accomplish and how long each task will take. Remember to add time for household jobs if you have them. Next, add in time to do the things you enjoy doing, activities you are involved in, family time, and friend time. Does everything fit? If so, great! If not, play around with the schedule to see how you can fit everything into it.

All these tools and strategies for organizing your time and assignments really do work. It might take some time or trial and error to figure out your preferred method of being organized, but it is worth the effort. However, if you hit a roadblock and aren't sure how to get it all done, don't be afraid to ask your parents, teachers, or older siblings for study strategies and organizational tips that have worked for them.

TAKING SHORTCUTS: YES OR NO?

Taking the easy or quick way to reach your goal isn't always a bad thing. Imagine if you and your family were driving to a vacation destination and your aunt told your parents about a more direct route that would get you there more quickly. Is there any down side to taking this shortcut? Probably not, unless the longer route had better scenery or passed a restaurant where you wanted to stop and eat.

But taking the shortcut for getting your schoolwork done can have some serious consequences, even though it may save you valuable time. What if you copied the math homework off of your friend, and your friend copied the social studies homework off of you? What are the problems with that shortcut? Problem number one is that your teacher might get suspicious and accuse you or your friend of not doing the work and trying to be deceitful, and who wants that? Problem number two is that you may not get enough practice or preparation for a test that is based on some of the concepts from the homework. Problem number three is that you might feel more confused in class and even feel embarrassed about what you are doing. It might even cause some conflicts between you and your friend if you decide to no longer copy the math, but your friend continues to ask for the social studies homework.

Another shortcut that can have serious consequences is something called plagiarism. Your teachers have probably talked to you about not copying from another kid during a test and not plagiarizing from a book or website. Plagiarism basically means that you take someone else's words and present them as yours. Lisette said, "I ran out of time to read a book for English class, so I just copied a review that I read about it. Boy do I regret that. I got in big trouble. I didn't think it was such a big deal at the time. Now I know better!"

> plagiarism basically means that you take someone else's words and present them as yours

It's sometimes hard to know how to put another person's ideas into your own words, even when you aren't trying to take a shortcut. Let's take a few minutes to discuss this, so that you don't accidentally get in trouble for plagiarizing. Jeffrey thought that the author of a book he was reading about Abraham Lincoln described him really well. Jeffrey said, "The author seems like an expert, so I wanted to use his words. I thought that was okay. I only used two sentences, but my teacher told me I plagiarized. I wasn't trying to cheat."

Jeffrey's teacher told him that if he had used a footnote—a note at the bottom of the page or at the end of the paper stating the author's name and the place where Jeffrey got his quote—he wouldn't have been plagiarizing. Basically, the rules are:

- Words that are copied exactly should always have quotes around them, and you should mention who said it and where you got the quote from.
- A sentence that you put in your report that is almost exactly the same as the one you read somewhere else should also have a footnote so the reader knows the idea and words basically came from another source.
- If you present someone else's words or specific ideas as your own, that is considered plagiarism.

If you aren't sure if you should quote and footnote, just check with your teacher *before* handing in your paper. It's a great way to learn and to have your questions answered. As a tween and a student, you are probably doing a lot more research projects than you used to and knowing this information is important for you now and for your future work.

Any time you think about taking a shortcut, think about the consequences—both external and internal. External consequences are what happen *to* you,

> any time you think about taking a shortcut, think about the consequences

such as your teacher giving you a low grade for the essay or your parents grounding you. Internal consequences are what happen *inside* you, such as feeling guilty or deprived of having learned important information. If you truly run out of time to do the project or study for the test, try talking with your teacher and parents about time management. Remember how Becca planned out her schedule for the week? At one point, her upcoming week was going to be overwhelmingly busy and she wasn't going to have enough time to study for her geography test. She shared her schedule with her parents, and together they came up with a solution: Becca reluctantly skipped her music lesson that week and didn't do her reading another night that week. Scheduling is like a puzzle. You try to fit all the pieces of your life into the week. If you run into problems, try to be creative and ask for help, rather than taking shortcuts that can backfire on you.

FINDING THE RIGHT STUDY ENVIRONMENT

After you have prioritized and organized your work and set up your schedule, the next task that tweens often work on is figuring out *how* and *where* to study. You may be told *what* you need to study for a test, but now that you are more independent as a tween, you may have several options to choose from about how and where to study. Think about whether you are better at preparing for tests when you study on your own or when you study in a group with friends (often called a study group). Do you end up daydreaming when you study alone? Do you get distracted by text messages and Instagram? Do you end up socializing and not focusing on the schoolwork when you are in a study group? Take a moment to think about this. There may be some subjects that you feel you must study alone and some that you want to try studying while in a study group.

Also spend some time thinking about where you study best. Do you work better when you are in your bedroom, sitting at a desk, with no distractions around you? Do you focus on your reading more when you lie down or sit up? Do you have trouble concentrating when you are in a quiet place? Are you the kind of student who works better at the library so you don't have any of the distractions you would have at home?

> spend some time thinking about where you study best

Here are some more questions to think about that may help you figure out *how, where,* and *when* you study best:

- Do the voices or activities in your home distract you? If so, it's time to find a quiet place.

- Do you benefit from having your parents nearby, even though you are doing most of the work independently? If so, find a good time and place—for example, before dinner at the kitchen table or in the family room— to get your work done with them nearby.

- Do you lose concentration after 20 minutes of studying, but usually have an hour's worth of homework? If so, can you break up the times into three 20-minute periods or just take a quick break every 20 minutes? Does that help?

- If you are a morning person, can you get up early to do some of your homework in the morning? This is tricky because you may need more time than you expect, and then might not finish before school. (It is probably better to do your work after you get home from school or during after-school study hall than in the morning or late at night.)

- If you are a night owl, can you take a break when you get home from school and start doing your homework a bit later? Keep in mind that if you start too late, you may end up interfering with your sleep time and end up tired the next day.

Learning *how, where,* and *when* you study best and what organizational strategies work best for you can help you in school now that you are a tween.

TWEEN
POINTS

- Any time you think about taking a shortcut, think about the consequences!

- Getting organized, prioritizing your work, and making a schedule may seem boring, but can eventually save you aggravation and time!

- Studying a little each day doesn't take more time than studying a lot at once, and it may feel less stressful!

In this chapter, you read about the ways that schoolwork may seem different in the tween years. In addition, organizational tips, study strategies, and the importance of avoiding some shortcuts, were explored.

CONCLUSION

As you continue on your journey through the tween years, you may find it helpful to review certain portions of this book to remember how other tweens have coped with certain changes and challenges. However, you are the only **you.** It's okay to find your own way to move from being a child to becoming a teenager.

ABOUT THE AUTHORS

WENDY L. MOSS, PhD, ABPP, FAASP, has her doctorate in clinical psychology, is a licensed psychologist, and has a certification in school psychology. Dr. Moss has practiced in the field of psychology for over 30 years and has worked in hospital, residential, private practice, clinic, and school settings. She has the distinction of being recognized as a diplomate in school psychology by the American Board of Professional Psychology for her advanced level of competence in the field of school psychology. Dr. Moss has been appointed as a fellow in the American Academy of School Psychology.

In addition, she is the author of *Bounce Back: How to Be a Resilient Kid; School Made Easier: A Kid's Guide to Study Strategies and Anxiety-Busting Tools,* with co-author Robin A. DeLuca-Acconi, LCSW; *Being Me: A Kid's Guide to Boosting Confidence and Self-Esteem;* and *Children Don't Come With an Instruction Manual: A Teacher's Guide to Problems That Affect Learners.* She has also written several articles. Dr. Moss is currently an ad hoc reviewer for the *Journal for Specialists in Group Work* and the *Journal of School Psychology.*

DONALD A. MOSES, MD, has his medical degree with a specialty in adolescent psychiatry. He is a licensed psychiatrist and has practiced in the field of psychiatry for over 40 years. He is on the staff of the North Shore University Hospital in Manhasset, New York, and was the psychiatric consultant to a substance abuse daycare center and a detoxification inpatient program. Dr. Moses was a flight medical officer in the United States Air Force, where he worked with flying personnel. In his private practice, he is distinguished as a specialist in helping tweens and adolescents to manage the stresses in their social, family, and academic lives, as well as to prevent and overcome substance abuse.

Dr. Moses is the author of *Are You Driving Your Children to Drink? Coping with Teenage Alcohol and Drug Abuse* and has published several articles. Dr. Moses has appeared on television as well as radio shows to discuss the topic of adolescent drug abuse and prevention.

ABOUT MAGINATION PRESS

MAGINATION PRESS is an imprint of the American Psychological Association, the largest scientific and professional organization representing psychologists in the United States and the largest association of psychologists worldwide.